Praise for
POWER NETWORKING

66 Power Networking *offers an extraordinary way to empower yourself and others as you create a community of support for yourself and your business.* 99

John Gray, Ph.D.
Author of *Men Are from Mars, Women Are from Venus*

66 *I recommend this book to anyone who wants to experience the joy and rewards of having a strong network of the right people.* 99

Andy Andrews
Entertainer/Author of *Storms of Perfection*

66 *A masterful job! I'm impressed with the clarity, focus, and wisdom.* 99

Alan Cohen
Author of *The Dragon Doesn't Live Here Anymore*

66 *Donna and Sandy reframe networking from a strategy to a deeply caring relationship. This book vividly illustrates the synergy of blending the best of people until the whole becomes transformed—far beyond the sum of its parts.* 99

Ann McGee-Cooper
Author of *You Don't Have to Go Home from Work Exhausted!* and *Time Management for Unmanageable People*

66 *Written from the hearts of two masters, it's a book that will stand the test of time. No man or woman who plans to be successful can be without what's in this book.* 99

John F. Demartini, D.C.
International speaker and author of *Top Performance Ideas for the Bottom Line Practice*

66 *A must for creating the success and prosperity you deserve.* 99

Anne Boe
Author of *Is Your "Net" Working?*

"Takes the skill and art of networking to new heights—provides practical information on how to develop your relationships to attain a new level of productivity, success, and pleasure in your personal and professional life."

Bob Schwartz
Author of *Diets Don't Work*, a *New York Times* Best-Seller

"Networking is a natural and effective marketing tactic when used properly. Donna and Sandy know networking—and how to teach networking to others."

Anthony O. Putman, Ph.D.
Author of *Marketing Your Services: A Step-by-Step Guide for Small Businesses and Professionals*

"Donna and Sandy's book is a great reminder of the power of people working together. It's refreshing to read of an approach to success based on thoughtfulness."

Susan RoAne
Keynote speaker and author of
How to Work a Room

"Networking is the highest form of service. It's people helping each other in a partnership destined for mutual benefit. Just one of the techniques in this book helped me land a contract of more than $21,000."

Joe Vitale
Author of *Turbocharge Your Writing*

"A brilliant example of how the universal principle of giving applies to the art of networking. You only get out of life what you give to others."

Douglas M. Lawson, Ph.D.
Fundraising consultant and
author of *Give to Live*

*"*Power Networking *captures the essence of what can be achieved by developing mutually supportive and trusting relationships."*

John Bradshaw
New York Times best-selling author of *Homecoming*

POWER
NETWORKING

---

55 Secrets for
Personal &
Professional Success

Donna Fisher and Sandy Vilas

MOUNTAINHARBOUR PUBLICATIONS

A BARD PRESS BOOK

Power Networking
55 Secrets for Personal & Professional Success

MountainHarbour Publications
1515 Capital of Texas Hwy S.
Suite 205
Austin, Texas 78746
512/329-8373   Fax 512/329-6051

Library of Congress Data 92-093405

Cloth edition ISBN 0-9627825-0-5
Trade paperback edition ISBN 0-9627825-4-8

First Edition

First printing	Aug 1991	Seventh printing	August 1996
Second printing	Oct 1991	Eighth printing	October 1997
Second Edition		Ninth printing	February 1999
First printing	July 1992		
Second printing	Dec 1992		
Third printing	Feb 1993		
Fourth printing	Mar 1994		
Fifth printing	Sept 1994		
Sixth printing	June 1995		

To order books or for information about workshops, seminars, presentations, and corporate trainings call the authors at:

Sandy Vilas
P.O. Box 881595
Steamboat Springs, CO
  80488-1595
1-970-870-3302
President@coachu.com
www.coachu.com

Donna Fisher
6524 San Felipe,
  Suite 138
Houston, Texas 77057
1-800-934-9675
Fishernet@aol.com
www.donnafisher.com

A BARD PRESS BOOK
Copyediting: **Helen Hyams**
Text Design: **Suzanne Pustejovsky**
Jacket Design: **Suzanne Pustejovsky**
Composition/Production: **Round Rock Graphics**
Indexing: **Linda Webster**

Visit our website @ www.bardpress.com

CONTENTS

Foreword by Marilyn Hermance   8

Acknowledgments   10

The Authors   12

1   We Believe in . . .   15

Part One

Eliminating the Roadblocks to Success

2   Beware the Networking Mongrel   21

3   Saying Goodbye to the Lone Ranger Mentality   23

4   No More Keeping Score   27

5   Facing the Fears   29

Part Two

Networking: Your Link to Success

6   So You're Not a Trapeze Artist   37

7   The Three P's of Networking: People, Power, and Promotion   39

8   Reaping the Benefits   43

9   Making a Small World Smaller   45

Part Three

The Power Networking Self-Assessment

10   The Self-Assessment   51
    Your Networking Profile

Part Four

The 55 Secrets

11 You Are the Hub of Your Network   59
    Know Your Own Power as a Networker

12 The Midas Touch   73
    Be Gracious and Courteous as You Network

13 The First Step–Rapport   93
    Handle Business Cards with Respect

14 A Thoughtful Person Is a Remembered Person   101
    Nurture Your Network with Acknowledgments

15 Maximize Your Actions   113
    Manage Yourself as a Resource

16 Ask and Ye Shall Receive   131
    Be Effective with Your Requests

17 It's Not Who You Know, It's Who Knows You   145
    Create Visibility Through Participation

18 Life Is Either a Daring Adventure or Nothing   155
    Develop a Personal Networking Approach

19 A Way of Life That Will Change the World   167
    Network to Enhance Your World

Part Five

A Lifestyle for Success

20 Planting the Seed   183

Bibliography   185
Index   187
Order Form/Speaker Inquiry   191

DEDICATION

To our network of family, friends, mentors, and associates

and

To the richness of life that comes from relationship,
friendship, and partnership

*66 Networking is making links from people we
know to people they know, in an organized way,
for a specific purpose, while remaining committed
to doing our part, expecting nothing in return.99*

Donna Fisher and Sandy Vilas

FOREWORD

In our business lives we meet people every day who are masters at finding one's Achilles' heel and exploiting that weakness to their own advantage.

And then . . . one meets people like Donna Fisher and Sandy Vilas, who look for and find the greatness in the people they meet. They encourage, acknowledge, and (sometimes) harass you into living up to your potential. For me, they are always there with a note or a phone call, or they just show up to keep me headed in the right direction.

Their real and amazing gift is that they teach this as a skill to others—a way of expanding not only the boundaries of friendships and contacts but also the boundaries of "seeing" and moving in the world.

Networking may be one of the buzzwords of the nineties but it is actually an old concept—"Do unto others."

The difference in networking as taught by Donna and Sandy is not that it describes how to broaden one's base of contacts but that it shows how to deepen all relationships. It is about seeing those old clichés—"going the extra mile," "taking the next step," and "what goes around comes around"—all come alive.

A group of sixty of us meet together every Friday morning. We are The Dover Club, a group of networking business people. We never talk about "tips" or "leads." We talk about small victories and big failures and about issues and concerns. We are able to stand up at 7:00 A.M. and talk about love and loss. Every week we acknowledge our committed support for each other. The support system I derive from this network has truly made it possible for me to do my job and be successful.

Largely because of Donna and Sandy, when we come together we always ask, "What do you need that I can help you with?" And even more astonishingly, we have learned to say, "This is what I need."

So welcome to the adventure of this book and to the adventure of what life can hold. It is probably not such a coincidence that an early group of networkers "worked with nets" and then spread a message of love to the world.

Marilyn Hermance
President, Custom Accessories

ACKNOWLEDGMENTS

To the many people who supported us in writing this book, we are deeply grateful. We give thanks to Bob Adler, Larry Andrews, Ray Bard, Bill Barron, Anne Boe, Pat Bradley, Steve Dailey, John Demartini, Alan Goldsberry, Ralph Hayes, Jessica Lipnack, Tim Marvin, Phil Morabito, Dana Morrison, Anthony Putman, Linda Schneider, Bob Schwartz, Janet Shorr, Gene Tognacci, and Judy West for reviewing various drafts of this book and responding with ideas, quotes, and encouragement. Your interest, support, and feedback helped us to make this book an expression of our belief in the power of networking. We also thank Catherine Noel, Laura Whitworth, and Tess Yevka for your friendship, loving support, and presence in our lives.

Special thanks to:

Amy Backlass, for your generous nature and loving support, as well as your technical expertise without which this book would not have been produced

Cindy Goldsberry, for responding with an enthusiastic yes anytime I asked for assistance

Linda Kay, for adding the new impetus, ideas, and energy that gave us just the boost we needed during the final phase of production

Thomas Leonard, for your magnificent coaching that has kept us on track, in momentum, and true to our dreams

Harvey Mackay, for your generous support and feedback and for being an example to us of the truth of our beliefs about networking

Joe Vitale, for your persistence with calls, notes, and clippings and for your continued expression of enthusiasm regarding our message

The present and past members of The Dover Club and The Windsor Club, for being the core network that supports us personally and professionally, serving as an extended family that we cherish, and exemplifying the truth that networking is about service, contribution, and support

Warmest regards,

Donna Fisher

Sandy Vilas

Photo by Evin Thayer

Donna Fisher, founder and president of Discovery Seminars of Houston, is a national authority on the importance of people skills, networking, and the personal touch in today's busy, topsy-turvy world. Her energetic platform style makes her a sought-after speaker at regional sales meetings, conventions, and international conferences, as well as a trainer at Hewlett-Packard, Merrill Lynch, Chevron, and other Fortune 500 companies.

Before forming her own company, Donna held sales, marketing, and management positions with Exxon, McDonnell Douglas Automation Company, the Houston Center for Attitudinal Healing, and the University of Houston. Author of the well-regarded book *People Power: 12 Power Principles to Enrich Your Business, Career, & Personal Networks,* she has been published and quoted in the *Wall Street Journal,* the *Chicago Tribune, Redbook, Executive Female,* and *Business Start-Ups*. Donna is one of thirteen women chosen from across the nation to be on the Business Owners Advisory Council of the American Business Women's Association.

Donna can be reached at 1-800-934-9675 or on her web site, www.donnafisher.com.

Sandy Vilas is president of Coach University, the world's largest training organization for personal and business coaches. Coach U has been featured in such publications as *Newsweek*, the *Times* of London, *Entrepreneur, Working Mother,* and *Inc.*, and on the NBC Nightly News with Tom Brokaw and CNN's Impact. Today it serves more than 2,500 students in 30 countries who are learning to help clients reach their personal and business goals.

Before becoming a key player in the personal and business coaching movement, Sandy was a successful training and sales consultant, delivering workshops and presentations to a wide range of clients across the country. Besides managing a ten-person staff at Coach U, Sandy continues to provide coaching services to his clients.

Sandy is an avid golfer and Harley rider. He lives in Steamboat Springs, Colorado. Sandy can be reached at 970-870-3302.

DECIDE TO NETWORK

Use every letter you write,
Every conversation you have,
Every meeting you attend
To express your fundamental beliefs and dreams.
Affirm to others the vision
Of the world you want.
Network through thought.
Network through love.
Network through the spirit.
You are the center of the network.
You are the center of the world.
You are a free, immensely powerful source
Of life and goodness.
Affirm it, spread it, radiate it.
Think day and night about it
And you will see a miracle happen:
The greatness of your own life.
Not in a world of big powers,
Media and monopolies,
But of five and a half billion individuals.
Networking is the new freedom,
The new democracy,
A new form of happiness.

Robert Muller
Former Assistant Secretary-General
United Nations

1

WE BELIEVE IN . . .

THE POWER OF NETWORKING

Networking creates a power that leads to a richer, fuller personal and professional life. When we speak of "power" networking we mean a power that comes from a spirit of giving and sharing. Personal power comes from an inner strength, from knowing who we are and what we have to offer, and from an awareness that we are part of a large and vast universe. Our power comes from our willingness to honor ourselves, our relationships, and our connection with the universal flow. It also comes from our ability to balance and integrate our dreams and goals with the people and opportunities around us. As Wayne Dyer says in *You'll See It When You Believe It,* "in a network the purpose is to give power away." We echo that theme throughout this book. We believe and know the many good things that can come from power networking in this spirit.

CHOOSING A WAY OF LIFE

Networking is the most cost-effective marketing tool around when it is used wisely, appropriately, and professionally. However, it is often misunderstood, misused, and therefore underused. We want to share our experiences and ideas with you so that networking can enrich your life in the same way it has enriched ours.

Our commitment is to teach and promote networking as a skill, a method of generating business, and a way of life that affects not only you, but the people around you and the world in which you live.

Networking is an attitude, an approach to life. It is not just a "thing to do." Instead it encompasses the way in which you relate to the people and the resources around you. Even though there are some specific skills and tools that you can learn about networking, unless you develop a power networking attitude, the impact is short-lived.

WHY NETWORK?

Networking has many benefits, but among the most important is that it is an efficient way to accomplish big goals! So if you have big goals and dreams about what you want to accomplish, power networking is for you. The bigger the goal, the more useful networking will be for reaching that goal. And with networking, you will attain success with greater ease, joy, and efficiency.

If you are not getting all you want out of life, then it is time to clarify your goals, fine-tune your focus, and strengthen and activate your network. Everyone has a vast network of resources already in existence; however, it is often forgotten, neglected, or ignored. Yet it can be rejuvenated. We want you to uncover your hidden network and nurture and build it to a new level of support, action, and results.

Did you know that

A referral generates 80 percent more results than a cold call?

Approximately 70 percent of all jobs are found through networking?

Most people you meet have at least 250 contacts?

Anyone you might want to meet or contact is only four to five people away from you?

No matter who you are, where you are, how old you are, or what profession you are in, you have vast resources available to you to accomplish whatever you want to accomplish in life.

If you're looking for another quick fix or magical solution to happiness and success, stop looking. You don't need a quick fix. Networking provides a solid foundation that lasts longer and produces greater results than any quick-fix idea ever could.

The secrets to success lie not in *what* you do but in *how* you do it and how well you work with others along the way. These secrets lie within you and depend on how you relate to yourself and the world around you. The key is to tap into your inner resources while working wisely with your outer resources: *your network*.

MORE THAN JUST A GOOD IDEA

It is our goal in our workshops to have people complete each day not only with good ideas but with the *experience* of having applied those ideas to enhance their life. We make sure that they practice what we are talking about throughout each workshop. And we encourage them to experiment with the information so that they personally discover how to apply it to their own goals.

This book is also designed to be much more than a review of good ideas. Instead, it is intended to be a catalyst to help you take action, build your network, and generate success. To make the best use of this material, we recommend that you read it, put it into practice immediately, and watch for results. The sections entitled "Plan Your Action; Act on Your Plan" are the working sections that give you specific instructions for implementing each idea into your life.

Most people have a tendency to get excited when they implement new ideas, but gradually, over time, they drift back into old habits, familiar patterns, and a predictable comfort zone. We encourage you to make an agreement with yourself to practice these ideas for at least thirty days and then let us know how it has made a difference in your personal and professional success.

How did networking become the focus of our life and our business? Here are some of the major events that directed us toward a networking lifestyle:

Sandy started his career as a stockbroker and quickly decided that cold calling was not what he wanted to do for the rest of his life. He developed his own style of exchanging leads, contacts, and referrals to generate business more quickly through "warm calls."

Soon after moving from North Carolina to Texas, Donna started a new career in sales. She found herself meeting a lot of people and generating new friendships and business relationships. She noticed how much this building of a new network of support helped in the transition to becoming part of a new community and moving forward with her professional goals.

Sandy found himself with a business that was trying to survive despite a sagging economy. The typical means of support were not adequate, so he founded a networking organization called The Dover Club that provided a strong foundation for personal and professional support.

As the executive director of the Houston Center for Attitudinal Healing, Donna discovered that making requests and being resourceful was not just a good idea but a vital aspect of working in the nonprofit sector. She developed a greater awareness of how much people want to help, participate, and contribute to one another.

These situations represent a chain of seemingly unrelated events that led to a decision to dedicate our lives to networking—to teach and promote networking as a positive, productive lifestyle that enhances the world through allowing people to connect and contribute to each other.

We believe in the ideas we are presenting to you because of our own experience. We believe in the opportunity to build a vast network of supportive relationships. We believe that people really want to contribute. We believe that we must take care of ourselves to truly be of service to others. We believe that networking is a way of relating to the world that will change your life and a way of life that will change the world and make the world a better place for all of us.

Networking has enriched our lives significantly and continues to do so daily. We are pleased to have the opportunity to live, teach, and share what we love.

This book will introduce you to many more than the "55 secrets," because it will instill in you a new way of thinking that supports you in using those "secrets" as the basis for a successful lifestyle. The information we are presenting to you can be the catalyst to start a lifelong process of establishing, building, and working with a mutually supportive network of relationships.

PART

One

ELIMINATING THE ROADBLOCKS TO SUCCESS

66 *Our greatest glory is not in never falling, but in rising every time we fall.* **99**

Confucius

2

BEWARE THE NETWORKING MONGREL

Networking mongrels are those people who have used and abused networking:

They collect a meaningless stack of business cards without ever connecting with the people.

They try to make the "sale" at a wedding, networking event, or first encounter.

They talk and focus on their agenda rather than listening with interest to gather information.

They intrude inappropriately and have short, superficial interactions.

They walk over people and forget the value of taking the time to establish relationship and rapport.

They get caught up in quantity rather than quality.

If you have had an unpleasant or uncomfortable networking experience, it is probably due to the abuse or misuse of the concept by a networking mongrel. Don't feel too bad if you notice that you have done some of the things listed above. That's why we are mentioning them—so that you will be more aware of the warning signs and can redirect your thoughts and actions before the mongrel ever surfaces.

Networking is *not:*

  Selling

  Using people strictly for your gain

  Coercing or manipulating someone to do what you want

  Putting friends, neighbors, or associates on the spot

  Badgering people about your business

Networking *is* the process of gathering, collecting, and distributing information for the mutual benefit of you and the people in your network. As Anthony Putman emphasizes in *Marketing Your Services* (1990, p. 171), "the purpose of networking is to *give* and *get* information. If you use networking properly, nobody feels pressured or used or put on the spot. *You are not selling, you are telling.* You are not asking for favors, you are giving valuable information."

Don't be a networking mongrel or you will turn people off and miss the magnificent opportunity of powerful networking. And if you run across mongrels as you are networking, simply let that be a reminder to fine-tune your power networking approach so that any mongrel tendencies are eliminated from your system.

Mongrel tendencies will keep you from fully maximizing the power of networking. However, a mongrel doesn't have to stay a mongrel, and it is possible to learn a new and better approach to networking. The best way to teach is by example. Through your own commitment to a positive networking approach, you can be a role model for others and can eliminate the misconceptions and abusive use of networking. Without the mongrel, networking can exist entirely as a powerful, positive experience of goodwill, trust, service, and contribution.

3

SAYING GOODBYE TO THE LONE RANGER MENTALITY

There is a prevalent and underlying idea in our culture that we are supposed to be superhuman beings who can accomplish major feats on our own, never asking for help and showing no sign of difficulty. We call this the "Lone Ranger mentality," that driving thought that we should know it all, have it all, always be the expert, and fearlessly do it all on our own. We could go on, but we think that's enough, don't you?

If you can finish the phrase "If you want a job done right, _ _ _ _ _ _ _ _ _ _ _," then you know what we are talking about.

Your attitude influences how you experience your day, your interactions with people, and the type of goals you set for yourself. It also affects your networking effectiveness. The Lone Ranger mentality is a major stumbling block for potential networkers. The bad news is that this attitude is ingrained in all of us to some degree. The good news is that you can choose to develop a new approach and say goodbye to the Lone Ranger mentality.

The following statements are examples of the Lone Ranger mentality. If you notice that any of these statements seem familiar to you, then beware of the tendency to operate on your own and disregard the support of others.

❏ I can do this by myself.

❏ I don't need anyone's help.

❏ I should already know how to do this.

❏ I know what needs to be done here.

❏ I don't want to bother people with . . .

❏ People are busy with their own work.

❏ People don't want to be bothered.

❏ I can't let others know I don't know how to do this.

❏ I shouldn't need anyone's help.

❏ I should be smart enough to figure this out myself.

❏ What will people think if I approach them about . . . ?

These statements are not truths; they are just thoughts. But if you have these thoughts, you are limiting yourself and blocking the full power, joy, and beauty of networking. Don't be a Lone Ranger! Instead of listening to limiting thoughts, you can choose thoughts that support a new and powerful approach to success:

❏ I can do this quickly and easily by working with the resources in my network.

❏ I enjoy having others contribute to me and help me with my goals.

❏ I am willing to learn new things from others.

❏ By working with others, I learn new and better ways to handle challenges.

❏ People appreciate the opportunity to contribute their expertise.

❏ People feel included and appreciated when I approach them for assistance or ideas.

❏ I am confident and feel okay about letting others know what I need.

❏ I am smart enough to use the resources and relationships in my network for support and assistance.

❏ People will think I am resourceful if I approach them with questions.

❏ Asking others' advice can help me in determining the best course of action.

❏ I am eager and enthusiastic about benefiting from the expertise and support of others.

These are powerful thoughts regarding an approach that empowers people to experience the best of who they are through networking.

Learning to be independent and do things on our own is an important step in the growing-up process. This is the stage in life in which we learn about our own values and strengths. However, this stage is meant to lead us to the more powerful stage of inner strength and interdependence. Our power as individuals comes not from our independence, but from our interdependence, our interactions, and the way we relate to the people and the opportunities around us. It is time to give up the Lone Ranger mentality and claim the power of people working together.

4

NO MORE
KEEPING SCORE

Networking consists of creating links from people we know to people they know in an organized way, for a specific purpose, while remaining committed to doing our part and expecting nothing in return. The key phrase here is the last part, "expecting nothing in return."

Expecting nothing in return means giving, contributing to, and supporting others without keeping score. Keeping score blocks the flow and makes people hesitant to give in return. Think about how you feel when you know that others are keeping track of what they have done for you and what they in turn think you owe them. You probably feel less inclined to network with them. And if you are the one keeping score, your focus may be more on the score than on the opportunity in front of you.

When someone has done something for you, don't you naturally want to reciprocate in some way? And isn't it much more enjoyable to do this of your own free will rather than from a place of obligation or fear? You don't have to make others feel obligated to support you. People naturally want to support each other, especially when trust, relationship, and respect are present. When trust exists, you don't need to worry about who gave to whom, or how often or how much they gave. When you trust people, you know that they will do the best they can, reciprocate when they can, and serve you in the same way that they have been served.

It may seem a little scary to give up keeping score, because then you can't use the scoreboard to control or influence people anymore. When no score is being kept, the focus is fully on building relationships and supporting people. You can't count on getting points for giving and contributing, but you can count on the quality and depth of your relationships.

This idea is not new at all, although it may be new for you to think of it in relation to networking. The idea has been expressed by the familiar sayings, "What goes around, comes around," "You reap what you sow," and "Give more than you expect to receive and you will get more than you ever need."

We call this concept the "boomerang effect." When you throw the boomerang it comes back, right? It doesn't return directly, but in its own roundabout way it does return to its place of origin. The same thing is true of networking. If you take the initiative to give, participate, and contribute, benefits will come back to you in some way, although they won't necessarily come back immediately from the same person. In fact, sometimes they will come back from totally unexpected places.

When you practice the boomerang effect, you may actually notice a sense of relief because you don't have to control things and keep score anymore. There is a newfound freedom when you can focus on your networking and allow the return to happen of its own accord. When you concentrate on supporting the other people in your network, you will receive an abundance of ideas, support, and referrals.

The heartbeat of networking is people caring about people. Even if you learn all the skills, say all the right things, and go through all the motions, networking is only truly powerful when genuine human caring exists.

5

FACING
THE FEARS

If networking is such a great marketing and promotional tool, why isn't it used more often? There are many fears and concerns that may automatically stop people from making that call, asking for that referral, or offering that support.

The value of networking is too great to allow these fears and concerns to get in the way. In addition, such fears and concerns are unfounded, because they are based on misconceptions about networking. See if your top fears are listed here, and take a fresh look at how your own attitude and approach to networking can generate these fears.

REJECTION

"I can't stand rejection!"

Of course, people don't like being turned down or rejected. Yet there is a new way to approach your networking interactions that eliminates rejection as an issue.

Networking consists of gathering, collecting, and distributing information. When you contact someone to let them know that you are looking for a referral, prospect, or service provider, you are giving that person information. Your focus is to distribute this information to a sufficient number of people to make the connections that will best serve you in reaching your goal and getting the support or contact that you want.

Rejection is an issue only if your focus is on having someone respond in a particular way. If you are relaying information primarily as a way to mutually share resources, then any response you get will support the flow of the process.

Networking is not about getting someone else to say or do what you want. Its purpose is to allow you to use the vast resources around you to further your goals. When you approach people as someone who is giving them information— for example, telling them about your current project or letting them know what type of support you are looking for—there is no rejection involved. You are simply giving them information to include in their networking data bank and have thus expanded your base of possible links.

OBLIGATION

"If they support me, what will they expect from me?"

"What if I can't give back to them to the same degree that they gave to me?"

Obligation doesn't feel good. It can be scary, burdensome, and troublesome. It touches on issues of being controlled, not being good enough, and feeling inferior. Yet, as we mentioned in Chapter Four, "No More Keeping Score," the power networking approach involves giving with no expectations and therefore no obligations (other than to treat people with mutual respect and appreciation).

If you use manipulation and intimidation to get what you want, your network will be shallow and your results sporadic. If you treat people with respect and give to the best of your ability, you will have done your part.

LOOKING WEAK OR NEEDY

"I don't want to look like I don't know what I'm doing."

"I need to look like I have it all together."

If your focus is to keep up a good front, you can't really network to your fullest potential. Some of the most rewarding and meaningful phone calls take place when someone calls and says, "I'm having difficulty with . . . What can you recommend?"

We consider "asking for support" as the smart approach to life. When people call us and tell us that they need help, we know that they are more interested in "working smart" than in working hard just to look good.

Everyone has times of need. To pretend that you don't only keeps you separate and distant from people. When you are not looking to your network for self-validation and you are focused on your goals, then appearing weak or needy need not be a concern.

There is an interesting dichotomy here. When people ask us for support we typically feel pleased, acknowledged, and honored that they thought of us and thought enough *of* us to feel that we could be of assistance. Isn't that true for you, too? By polling the people in our workshops, we have found that this is consistently true. Yet isn't it interesting that so few people ask for what they want or need!

It is important to realize that asking for support is not a sign of weakness but really an indication of

Strong self-esteem

A commitment to the goal rather than the ego

A willingness and ability to learn from others

The wisdom to be inclusive rather than exclusive

The willingness to let things happen easily rather than reinventing the wheel each time

An understanding of the power of interdependence

Asking for support is an important part of networking. Asking is not a sign of weakness; on the contrary, it is a sign of strength, courage, and wisdom.

SPENDING TOO MUCH TIME

"I don't have time to network."
"I already have more than I know how to handle."

Reinventing the wheel, trying to sell through cold calling, and tackling your projects by yourself take too much time. With networking, it is possible to accomplish much more in less time. We are not promoting networking as another "thing to do." You probably already have plenty to do. Instead, we teach networking as a way to enhance what you are already doing.

Networking does not mean that you have to spend time looking for new opportunities. In fact, it's just the opposite. Through networking you will be more aware of opportunities and will be able to maximize each interaction and leverage more effectively with the contacts you already have.

Networking requires you to be aware. If you are not networking, you can end up spending more time and money on activities that could have been done more efficiently by working with your resources. When you talk to people, network; when you ride the elevator, network; when you call on a client, network. Be smart with your time and integrate networking into what you are already doing.

APPEARING PUSHY AND AGGRESSIVE

"If it means having to be pushy and aggressive, I can't do it."

Networking requires patience and persistence just like planting a seed, nurturing it, and waiting for it to grow. However, showing persistence tempered with patience is very different from being pushy and aggressive. You don't have to be pushy or aggressive to get results, although it is important to participate and interact with people. But you can network in a way that is comfortable and a natural fit for your own personal style.

If you are demanding or overbearing, you have slipped into what we call the "networking mongrel" role (covered in Chapter Two). This can happen if you lose sight of the big picture and are caught up in thinking that there is only one avenue toward reaching a goal. Remember that a multitude of resources are available through your network and that your focus is to build strong relationships. In those relationships you will find the people who *want* to support you. As your network becomes strong you will find that more and more people offer support before you ever get around to asking.

BEING COLD AND IMPERSONAL

"Networking seems impersonal, forced, and cold."

"I don't want to be one of those people who is always out to get something for himself."

Networking will only seem impersonal if there is no focus on relationships and the only agenda is to get results. Anyone who approaches people in this way will find her network fizzling before it ever has a chance to become strong.

Networking is the genuine expression of interest in others and the willingness to contribute and support them when possible. If your interactions are natural and authentic, your own openness and vulnerability will lead to strong relationships and more satisfying interactions. The power of networking comes from people and the development of strong, solid relationships.

As you can see, all of these fears lose their power when you are operating from a power networking approach. Networking can be fun, exciting, satisfying, and rewarding. It is your approach and attitude that will make the difference and dissolve the fears that have gotten in your way in the past.

PART

NETWORKING:
YOUR LINK
TO
SUCCESS

66 *If you want to be prosperous for a
year, grow grain.
If you want to be prosperous for
ten years, grow trees.
If you want to be prosperous for a
lifetime, grow people.* **99**

Proverb

6

So You're Not a
Trapeze Artist

If you were a trapeze artist, you would make sure that your safety net was in place, solid, strong, and working, wouldn't you? A trapeze artist uses a safety net for obvious reasons—the risk is too great not to. This net allows the artist to take chances, learn new routines, practice without getting hurt, and build confidence.

Even though you're not a trapeze artist, you also take risks. Whether you're an entrepreneur, sales representative, or chief executive officer, you take risks all the time. And when you have big dreams and goals, you're taking even bigger risks. Just like the trapeze artist, you should have a strong, solid net working for you!

Is Your "Net" Working? is the title of a book written by Anne Boe and Bettie Youngs (1989), and the title itself is priceless and worth pondering. Is your net working? Are the links strong and the connections solid? Is it set up to provide the type of support you want and need? Are you taking good care of it?

Life can sometimes make you feel as if you're jumping from a trapeze, floating in midair, or taking a leap of faith. Your network can be your safety net, your moral support, and your backup system when you

Make a job transition

Move to a new city

Start your own business

Change career paths

Decide to expand your business

Are you doing the things you really want to do with your life? Are you taking the "leaps of faith" required to accomplish your dreams? If you are not taking the risks necessary to do the things you really want to do in life, your first step should be to build and develop your network. A net that is working provides the backup and support you need to step out and do the things you want to do with your business and your life.

THE THREE P'S OF NETWORKING:
POWER, PEOPLE, AND PROMOTION

Networking is a universal principle that is in motion all around the world. The power of this principle is not just that it is universal but that it generates far-reaching results and is accessible to all people. There are no limiting criteria, for the power of networking does not depend on your age, educational degree, financial status, career path, or geographic preference. The power of networking is available to anyone and everyone, at least to anyone who is willing to consistently and extensively contribute to people through the mutual sharing of resources.

"Power networking," as we refer to it, is an approach that encompasses all areas of life, generates fulfillment and satisfaction at a deep level, and links people together for a surge of productive energy.

The power of networking is not defined by how much is gained from others, but rather by the human interaction and the personal value generated by the interaction. Anything you can think of that you have accomplished includes other people. Whether it was something as simple as sending a letter across town or as complex as sending a person to the moon, it required many people and many relationships to produce the result.

Power networking is being skillful not only in generating business but in enhancing your business and life for the greater good of all.

The following statements express the ideas of people from all walks of life regarding what networking means to them. Notice that each definition is unique, and yet they all have a common underlying theme—people—who are promoting, empowering, supporting, nurturing, connecting, and relating to other people. The common ingredient in any positive networking interaction is that of people empowering people. This is where the heart and power of networking reside. We encourage you to write a definition for yourself that expresses in your own words the focus and value of networking in your life.

66 Networking is a communication process—exchanging information and receiving advice and referrals. 99

Ronald L. Krannich and Caryl Rae Krannich
Network Your Way to Job and Career Success

66 Networking means sending out into the system what we have and what we know, and having it return to recirculate continually through the network. 99

Wayne Dyer
You'll See It When You Believe It

66 Creating relationships whereby you can help others achieve their goals, which in turn will help you achieve yours. 99

Ralph Hayes
President, Data Voice Technologies

66 Networking is people connecting with people, linking ideas and resources. 99

Jessica Lipnack and Jeffrey Stamps
The Networking Book

❝ *The systematic process of meeting people, learning about them, and establishing relationships so that all parties establish and expand a base of resources to support their endeavors.* **❞**

John Hoppe
President, Independence Capital Company

❝ *Communication that creates the linkage between people and clusters of people.* **❞**

John Naisbitt
Megatrends

❝ *Networking is establishing connections that are mutually satisfying, helpful, and uplifting.* **❞**

H. S. Khalsa
EcoWater Systems

Networking, like a coin, has two sides, and you can't have one side without the other. Networking is about results and relationships, effectiveness and efficiency, graciousness and persistence. It encompasses trusting and requesting, generating business and promoting others, giving information and accepting support.

Power Networking Is About:

Results	*and*	Relationships
Effectiveness	*and*	Efficiency
Assertiveness	*and*	Graciousness
Persistence	*and*	Trusting
Promoting yourself	*and*	Promoting others
Building your business	*and*	Enhancing your life
Receiving	*and*	Giving
Accepting support	*and*	Contributing
Requesting	*and*	Offering

8

REAPING THE BENEFITS

As John Naisbitt explains in his book *Megatrends* (1982, p. 192), "Networks exist to foster self-help, to exchange information, to change society, to improve productivity and work life, and to share resources." Networking can be applied to situations in all areas of life as a means to

Collect and distribute information to people effectively

Produce major results with ease and efficiency

Share leads, ideas, and expertise with others

Connect people with one another

Accomplish goals through the power of synergy

Verify the accuracy and validity of information and ideas

Promote a product, service, or idea

Increase productivity by making wise use of resources and opportunities

Create greater results in less time through maximization of interactions and conversations

Whether you want to provide a service, buy a product, meet a new associate, or find a job, networking can be the process that enhances your chance for success. As noted by Marilyn Ferguson, author of *The Aquarian Conspiracy* (1981, pp. 62–63), the process of networking can be done by "conferences, phone calls, air travel, books, phantom organizations, papers, pamphleteering, photocopying, lectures, workshops, parties, grapevines, mutual friends, summit meetings, coalitions, tapes, newsletters."

Just as there are many ways to network, there are many benefits to reap. From monetary gain to personal satisfaction, the benefits of networking will touch all areas of your life:

Networking provides easier access to products and services.

Networking enhances teamwork and camaraderie.

Networking provides opportunities for mutual sharing, serving, supporting, and giving to one another.

Networking generates ease, fun, and success in all endeavors.

Networking provides a socially acceptable way to contribute to people.

Networking leads to new relationships, new opportunities, and greater accomplishments.

Networking provides opportunities for expanding our horizons on a personal and professional level.

Networking assists in the realization of our goals and dreams in life.

Networking fulfills the basic human desire for relationship, satisfaction, and service.

The benefits of networking will add richness to your life personally and professionally. And the degree to which you reap these benefits will be in direct correlation to the degree to which you participate and use networking effectively in your life. When you give, contribute, participate, and support others, these deeds will come back to you and you will enjoy the harvest of networking's multitude of benefits.

9

MAKING A SMALL WORLD SMALLER

How many times have you said or heard someone say, "It's a small world, isn't it?" Networking is what makes the world "small" enough so that people are within our reach and connections can be made readily and often. How many times have you thought that something happened because you were fortunate enough to be "in the right place at the right time"? Perhaps it wasn't just happenstance, but the result of effective networking. By learning to network effectively throughout your life, you will create your own "luck" that puts you "in the right place at the right time." Through a networking approach to life you can enjoy the personal satisfaction of a "small world" along with the rich benefits of a large and technologically expanding world.

When you integrate networking into your life, you are developing a skill that will serve you forever and connect you with people globally. As we have indicated, networking is a universal concept that happens on a daily basis all around the world:

Jim tells Lisa about the new restaurant in town.

Tim gives Robert a contact for a new job opportunity.

Betty gives Linda the name and number of her favorite caterer.

Roy introduces Randy to the president of his professional association.

Susan sends Alan an article with information that could be used for the book he is writing on advancements concerning environmental issues.

Becky asks Steve for the name of a graphic designer who can help her with business cards and stationery for her new business.

Phil contacts Mark to tell him to expect a call from his client, Ken, who could be a potential investor in Mark's new clinic.

Mike invites Larry to play golf with his Japanese associates who are in town on business.

After making a presentation to the Marketing Executives' Association, John gives the program chairperson the names and numbers of three well-qualified speakers for the organization.

This list obviously could go on and on. In any city, town, or community, however large or small, people know about networking, whether they call it networking, helping, support, or simply friendship. Think back to the history of our country and the stories you have heard about barn raisings, quilting bees, and bartering. Throughout time and in all walks of life, people have used networking to accomplish individual, group, and community goals.

Over the last decade, our mobile society has changed significantly, leaving many people without the normal support of a close network of families and neighborhoods. People have adjusted to this shift by creating new families of support to satisfy their desire for bonding, camaraderie, and belonging.

Grass-roots organizations have made major strides in creating social and environmental changes in our society. These organizations are prime examples of powerful networking. People of like mind rally behind a cause, spread the word, and gather information, resources, and support. They often expand rapidly in numbers and strength, thus generating the momentum and energy that ends up producing a result with greater ease and less expense than would be possible for a bureaucratic organization. When traditional structures fail, people will reach out to one another and start a cluster. These clusters become a network and the network becomes a vehicle that addresses the needs and desires of the people as individuals, in their community, and in their society.

Advances in telecommunications and computer technology are increasing the ability to network faster all around the world in a more sophisticated way. Networking has become a necessary tool for dealing with the large volume of information and resources with which we are inundated today. Ten years ago John Naisbitt, in his best-seller *Megatrends* (1982, pp. 192–193), identified networks as "structured to transmit information in a way that is quicker, more high touch, and more energy-efficient than any other process we know." Ever since then, technological improvements have advanced networking to a new level of speed, sophistication, and efficiency.

While networking becomes easier and more prominent, it is at the same time important to keep the "heart" of networking present. Whether you are talking with people in person or through machinery, whether they are friends who live next door or contacts on the other side of the globe, you have the ability to convey friendship, support, and relationship through your interaction.

People everywhere are joining networking organizations, attending networking trainings and seminars, hiring networking consultants, and using their networks to find jobs. Individuals are becoming known as "networkers" and employers are expressing an interest in hiring people who bring with them an already established pool of resources. There is an increase in the number of networking books and tapes being published, as well as in networking trainings, college courses, consultants, and organizations.

John Naisbitt (1982, p. 192) brought to people's attention the idea that "the new networking model . . . is replacing the hierarchical form we have grown to associate with frustration, impersonality, inertia, and failure." In their book *Is Your "Net" Working?* (1989, p. 27), Anne Boe and Bettie Youngs predict that networking "will be an even more essential skill in the future." The power of networking, the advances in technology, and the shifting structure and interests of our society are all contributing to the increased popularity and usefulness of networking. We predict that this focus on networking will explode over the next decade.

We expect to see networking's popularity gain even greater momentum because, through networking, people satisfy their achievement and affiliation needs by working with a support system that is as large, small, or expansive as they wish. The affectionate nature of networking warms the heart and spirit, the ease and efficiency with which things are accomplished serves the body, and the results that are produced stimulate and reward the mind. A networking lifestyle is a well-rounded approach that nurtures and satisfies people in a deep and meaningful way.

Affection.   Networking provides affection because it is made up of people relating to people. People appreciate the opportunity to support each other. It satisfies our natural desire to be of service, to contribute, and to experience the warmth of family and friendship.

Efficiency.   Networking is efficient because we use the skills, strengths, and expertise of others. Through networking, we bypass the mistakes and pitfalls that others have encountered. We are able to gain from the wisdom of others and produce results with greater ease and efficiency.

Powerful results.   Networking produces powerful results because the synergy of people interacting and supporting each other generates action, and directed action leads to results. The energy generated by people who are networking in a positive, productive, and powerful manner will create sparks of activity that ripple throughout their network.

Networking has been around forever and it always will be. Don't let it seem like just a happenstance in your life. The potential of networking is that it can be used by everyone for projects and endeavors in all areas of life. Learn to network and you will have a powerful approach to life that will always serve you!

PART

THE POWER
NETWORKING
SELF-ASSESSMENT

66 *Power comes through cooperation,
independence through service, and a
greater self through selflessness.* **99**

John Heider
The Tao of Leadership

CHAPTER

10

THE SELF-ASSESSMENT

Our goal is to inspire you to be a power networker and enjoy the benefits and satisfaction of networking in your daily life. Whether you consider yourself a novice, intermediate, or expert networker, there is room for enhancement. The networking profile that follows will help you identify to what extent you are currently practicing the principles, tools, techniques, and attitude of a powerful networker. It will also reinforce the ideas you already practice, present new tools for greater effectiveness, and identify the steps you can take to achieve consistent networking success.

To determine your networking profile, score yourself on a scale of 1 to 5 (1 = never, 2 = occasionally, 3 = regularly, 4 = frequently, 5 = always) in terms of how each statement applies to the way you currently live your life. Be honest with yourself. This is your opportunity to assess your present level of expertise before you start on a path to a new and exciting world of networking.

When you complete the series of statements, total your score and check to see where you rated yourself on the scale from Lone Ranger to power networker. You may notice that you have been a Lone Ranger most of your life or that you have already developed expertise and mastery in the area of networking.

The networking profile consists of nine sections that correspond to Chapters Eleven through Nineteen of this book. In these chapters, each statement is explained with information, ideas, and examples. Personal stories show how these ideas have made an impact on the lives of people just like you.

Wherever you are today, you can develop new habits, enhance your skills, and integrate proven networking concepts into your life. Review the information in Chapters Eleven through Nineteen regarding each statement and begin your process of networking enhancement right now!

YOUR NETWORKING PROFILE

Rate yourself on a scale of 1 through 5.

1 = never   2 = occasionally   3 = regularly   4 = frequently   5 = always

Know Your Own Power as a Networker

_____   1. I know the values and principles that are important in my life.

_____   2. I can list five major accomplishments that I am proud of in my life.

_____   3. I am clear about my expertise and the resource I can be for others.

_____   4. I have given up the Lone Ranger mentality.

_____   5. I know my own power as a networker.

_____   6. I have a written list of long- and short-term goals that I review and revise regularly.

_____   7. I have a network diagram that represents the magnitude and diversity of my network.

Be Gracious and Courteous as You Network

_____   8. My presentation professionally represents who I am and what I do.

_____   9. I introduce myself in a way that is clear, concise, and personable, and that generates interest.

_____   10. I am at ease in groups and use conversation generators effectively.

_____   11. I reintroduce myself to people rather than waiting for them to remember me.

_____   12. I focus on people as they are introduced to me so that I remember their name and who they are.

_____   13. I am comfortable playing host at networking events.

_____   14. I am comfortable promoting and creating visibility for myself and my business.

_____   15. I am gracious and courteous with everyone I meet.

Handle Business Cards with Respect

_____ 16. My business cards are attractive and representative of who I am and what I do.

_____ 17. I have sufficient business cards handy for each situation.

_____ 18. I give out my business cards appropriately.

_____ 19. I make notations on business cards that I receive as memory joggers and follow-up reminders.

Nurture Your Network with Acknowledgments

_____ 20. I receive and give acknowledgments daily.

_____ 21. I acknowledge the people who inspire me whether or not I personally know them.

_____ 22. I nurture my network with calls, notes, and gifts in a timely and appropriate manner.

_____ 23. I have personalized notecards.

_____ 24. I graciously receive and accept acknowledgment and support.

Manage Yourself as a Resource

_____ 25. I have established an effective system for organizing and retrieving my network.

_____ 26. My business card file is organized and up to date.

_____ 27. I use a time management system effectively.

_____ 28. My daily action list is completed each day with items transferred or checked off.

_____ 29. I do what is in front of me rather than creating more items on my action list.

_____ 30. I return phone calls within twenty-four hours.

_____ 31. I organize my thoughts before making a phone call to referrals, leads, or people in my network.

_____ 32. I say no to events, activities, and meetings that drain my time, energy, or focus.

_____ 33. I prepare for networking events in order to maximize the opportunity.

Be Effective with Your Requests

_____ 34. I ask for and use the support of others.

_____ 35. I make requests of my network in a clear, concise, and nondemanding manner.

_____ 36. I consistently find opportunities to ask, "Who do you know who . . . ?"

_____ 37. I follow up promptly on leads.

_____ 38. I gain value from every contact.

Create Visibility Through Participation

_____ 39. I am a member of a professional organization.

_____ 40. I serve on a committee or board of an organization.

_____ 41. I regularly give referrals to and make requests of my network.

_____ 42. I am aware of and use the "three-foot rule."

_____ 43. I consistently reevaluate and add to my network.

Develop a Personal Networking Approach

_____ 44. I trust and follow my intuition.

_____ 45. I am committed to the success of the people in my network.

_____ 46. I am known for the high level of service I provide.

_____ 47. I am an active and perceptive listener.

_____ 48. I operate with integrity and professionalism in all my interactions and endeavors.

_____ 49. I approach each contact and opportunity with an open mind.

Network to Enhance Your World

_____ 50. I am known as a powerful networker with an established and resourceful network.

_____ 51. I use networking to benefit myself and others personally as well as professionally.

_____ 52. I keep my network in the forefront of my thinking.

_____ 53. I am a role model for power networking.

_____ 54. I see the world as one big network.

_____ 55. Networking is a way of life for me.

Scores:

275–237 Powerful
236–200 Effective
199–164 Resourceful
163–128 Branching out
127–92   Timid
 91–55   Lone Ranger

PART
Four

THE 55 SECRETS

*66Knowledgeable people know facts.
Successful and prosperous people know
people.99*

John Demartini

11

YOU ARE THE HUB OF YOUR NETWORK: KNOW YOUR OWN POWER AS A NETWORKER

1 KNOW THE IMPORTANT VALUES AND PRINCIPLES IN YOUR LIFE.

66Fulfillment is essentially a relationship between yourself and your personal values and conscience.99

John F. Raynolds III and Eleanor Raynolds
Beyond Success

The first step in becoming a powerful networker is to get your own life in order and orient your life around the values and principles that are important to you. Your values consist of the qualities that are the core of life for you, those that make your life worthwhile and give it meaning and satisfaction.

Values are qualities such as:

Adventure	Freedom	Joy
Appreciation	Fun	Love
Beauty	Harmony	Order
Certainty	Honesty	Participation
Comfort	Honor	Peace
Communication	Humor	Pleasure
Contribution	Independence	Power
Control	Integrity	Recognition
Creativity	Intimacy	Respect
Discovery		Spirituality

Although all of these values may be important to you, there are certain ones that are key and essential in your life. When you are aware of *your* top values (not the values that you think you should have), you will possess a more solid foundation from which to relate to yourself and others.

Many people go through life setting goals, building careers, and undertaking projects that are impressive and yet not satisfying. This is because they have not oriented their life around the goals, projects, and careers that fulfill their values.

With value-based goals, there is a natural motivation that propels you to action. Once your life and your goals are designed around your values, you will have a clearer sense of yourself, which will provide strength and certainty to enhance your networking focus.

2 LIST FIVE MAJOR ACCOMPLISHMENTS THAT YOU ARE PROUD OF IN YOUR LIFE.

66 *Whosoever knows others is clever.*
Whosoever knows himself is wise. **99**

Lao Tzu
Tao Te Ching

Everything you do—mailing a letter, setting up a luncheon meeting, coordinating a sale—depends on the resources and participation of others. There are support people around all the time contributing to your everyday activities as well as your major accomplishments. Being aware of this will reinforce your appreciation of networking as a natural and effective part of your life.

Your accomplishments provide valuable information about who you are as a networker and what type of resources you have to offer to others. If you are a marathon runner, you have expertise and contacts to share regarding training for a marathon. If you have written a book, you have the knowledge, experience, and contacts that would support anyone who is considering writing a book. It is important that you share your accomplishments so that the expertise, contacts, and experience you gained can be of benefit to others.

If you do not let others know what you have accomplished, they will not know to call on you for support. Sharing your accomplishments will help you find opportunities to teach others what you have learned, which is part of the process of networking. By recalling your accomplishments, you can consciously see where to position yourself to be a resource for others. If you have a musical background, you can join a choral group, volunteer for a local theater group, or participate on the committee for the annual city music festival. You can build on your accomplishments and at the same time expand and utilize your network. You will also discover that your skills will strengthen when you teach others what you have learned.

You know what is important to you. You are the only one who really knows the significance of each accomplishment in your life. Be proud of all your accomplishments, whether they seem small, large, significant, easy, or difficult.

It is up to you to empower and acknowledge yourself and celebrate your accomplishments. Keeping your accomplishments in the forefront of your thinking will help you remember to network and share the benefits and expertise of your successes with others.

BE CLEAR ABOUT YOUR EXPERTISE AND THE RESOURCE YOU CAN BE FOR OTHERS.

❝ *The only gift is a portion of thyself.* ❞

Ralph Waldo Emerson
Gifts

Networking involves both giving of yourself as a resource and recognizing others for the resource that they are. Clarity about your own strengths, skills, talents, and expertise will assist you in being of service to others. As a power networker you will have to give up being a "closet" expert.

Everyone has special skills and abilities that can be useful to others. Do what you do well for yourself and others; allow others to do what they do well for you. When we each fit into a niche, everyone is served and all the pieces of the puzzle fit together.

In defining your expertise identify what you are

Adept at

Experienced with

The source of

Trained in

Natural with

Often people have skills that are so natural for them that they lose sight of the value of these skills. It is easy to think that something you do well is simple and easy for everyone else, but this is not necessarily true. What is natural for you may be confusing and difficult for someone else. Allow your natural talents and abilities to be the gift you give to your network.

GIVE UP THE LONE RANGER MENTALITY.

**❝ *We can't look out for 'number one'
because there is no number one! The
world is a team.* ❞**

Ron McCann and Joe Vitale
The Joy of Service

As we indicated in Chapter Three, many of us grew up hearing the phrase "If you want a job done right, do it yourself." This phrase represents the attitude that we call the "Lone Ranger mentality." The Lone Ranger mentality exemplifies the belief that we must know it all, do it the best, not show any weaknesses, and not let anyone else know when we need help. This thinking, however, is exactly what gets in the way of our being powerful and effective as networkers.

It is never too late to give up the Lone Ranger mentality and develop a power networker approach. However, it is a conscious choice that you must make, followed by developing new habits, new ways of thinking, and a new networking lifestyle.

No matter how long or how often you have demonstrated the Lone Ranger mentality, you can give it up and choose to develop a power networker approach.

To Move from Lone Ranger to Power Networker:

❑ Give up thinking that *you* have to be the expert.

❑ Notice when you are trying to handle things all by yourself.

❑ Be vulnerable and ask for help.

❑ Delegate to others.

❑ Let people know that you do not have all the answers.

❑ Become a team player.

❑ Accept and express appreciation of the support and contributions of others.

The Lone Ranger mentality is a common stumbling block to becoming a successful networker. When you are in need of information, support, or ideas, do you ask for what you want or do you try to figure things out for yourself? Break out of the Lone Ranger mold and you will find a whole new world of networking relationships and opportunities.

5 KNOW YOUR OWN POWER AS A NETWORKER.

66 *What one man can do is change the world and make it new again.* **99**

John Denver
As quoted in Alan Cohen, *The Healing of the Planet Earth*

To be powerful as a networker you must acknowledge and appreciate the power of networking and your own power as a networker. If you say, "But I don't know anyone!" or "I can't be of help to them," or "I don't have anything to contribute," then you will miss out on opportunities to network and support others.

People often slight their own contributions and accomplishments, but as a networker you must accept, acknowledge, and trust yourself. Through your own commitment to network, you will discover the power you have to offer. You probably contribute to others more than you realize. Allow yourself to begin to experience and enjoy the contributions you make.

Begin to notice the vast resource of contacts you have made and the wealth of skills and experiences you have gathered over your lifetime. Think of yourself as a powerful resource, give up limited thinking, and develop "possibility thinking." As a power networker, you should look for opportunities to contribute your ideas and contacts. When people make requests of you, respond as a resource rather than as an individual and you will unleash the power of your network.

Networking power is bestowed on you by your network through participation, selfless contribution to others, and the consistent demonstration that you care about the success of your network.

Networking is a form of teamwork, and the joy of teamwork is that everyone can benefit from and celebrate everyone else's success. The more you experience the joy and power of networking, the more you will grow as a networker.

6 HAVE A WRITTEN LIST OF LONG- AND SHORT-TERM GOALS THAT YOU REVIEW AND REVISE REGULARLY.

66 The list makers of the world are on the right track because they have at least set out to do something. 99

Emily Kittle Morrison
Skills for Leadership

It is difficult to reach a destination without a map, just as it is impractical to approach a project without a plan that identifies its purpose, goals, and objectives. The act of listing and reviewing your goals will help you to stay on track and realize how you can network effectively to accomplish these goals.

By writing your goals, you will gain greater clarity, conviction, and power, which will support you in attaining these goals. When you share your goals with others, you will further enhance your own commitment and focus and create a degree of accountability.

As a power networker your goals will become a source of direction, fulfillment, and self-expression. Your ability to communicate your goals very specifically will help others know how to network with you to make those goals become a reality.

7   HAVE A NETWORK DIAGRAM THAT REPRESENTS THE MAGNITUDE AND DIVERSITY OF YOUR NETWORK.

> **66** *Structurally, the most important thing about a network is that each individual is at its center.* **99**
>
> **John Naisbitt**
> *Megatrends*

A network diagram provides a visual representation of the magnitude and diversity of your network. To draw your diagram, take a single sheet of paper and write your name in the middle of the page as the hub of your network. From this hub, draw lines representing the major spokes of your network (family, business associates, clubs, church, alumni, and so on). Each spoke has branches for the key individuals in each of these major areas. This diagram provides a new level of organization and a greater awareness of the resources you have available to you.

Your network diagram can serve as a memory jogger for new or current opportunities. Whenever you start a new project or are looking for the right people to ask for specific support, your diagram can help you to identify, plan, and implement your networking approach. When you want to contact a particular individual, look at your diagram to see who can be the link to help you make that contact.

Your network is actually three-dimensional; it is an intricate web of branches that link one network to another at all levels. Although you are at the center of your network, you are at the same time a spoke or branch for every person in it. Your network diagram is only a simplified representation of a dynamic, powerful, and elaborate structure.

Just as your network will grow and change with time, your network diagram will grow, change, and develop new branches and directions throughout your life. Your diagram can continue to serve as a reminder of the magnitude and expansiveness of your network and the powerful role that you play as its center.

NETWORKING —IN— ACTION

Follow Your Heart–Julie Devodier

Julie Devodier found herself at a point in her life where she had a good job and income; yet she still felt as if something was missing. She yearned to leave it all and do something else, even if it seemed totally irrational to her family and friends.

Julie knew in her heart that there was something else for her, so she reached out for help. Through a coaching session, she discovered her top values in life and identified her life purpose. This provided her with clarity and answers to why she was not happy in her career, but most importantly it confirmed what she had known in her heart.

After getting back in touch with her values, Julie began to speak about what she wanted to do with her life. She was immediately referred to two people; two months later, through one of these contacts, Julie was being trained as a "ropes" consultant. She worked on an outdoor ropes course where people participate in exercises that use ropes and telephone poles to teach teamwork, problem resolution, and self-esteem. Several months later, Julie met two people with whom she became partners in starting a new company, called "What's Possible," which offered ropes courses to businesses and corporations.

These were major steps for Julie toward fulfilling her dream, which was to support people in their personal development. And it fulfilled all of her values:

Love of nature	The ropes courses are held outdoors.
Adventure	Each day brings a new opportunity to work with people and create adventure for others.
Loyalty	A business partnership was created that is based on respect and accountability.

Teamwork	There is a team experience with the business partners, and during a ropes course, "the whole day *you are a team!*"
Order/organization	The business must be organized effectively, keeping track of such details as promotions, registrations, equipment, and contracts.

Julie's clarity about her values and goals in life gave people the opportunity to network with her to further her dream. The difference for her in her new work is the thought *"This is me!"* and the realization that "the quality of life, joy, and peace" that she now has is what was missing previously. "I had never before believed so wholeheartedly in what I was doing that I could easily and naturally tell others about it." Julie found that being true to her heart has made it easy to promote and network her new business.

With the Help of Our Friends– Donna Fisher

When our workshop participants began asking for audiotapes, we realized that it was time to start on our first recording project. Having never produced audiotapes, we weren't quite sure where to begin, but we knew that we wanted to make it as quick, simple, and enjoyable as possible.

One day while talking to my girlfriend, Tess, I mentioned that I was trying to figure out how to do a recording project. She immediately responded, "Why don't you let me set you up to record at our studio!?" (She is a video producer and I realized that I had slipped into the Lone Ranger mentality, because here was a best friend with the resources to assist us and I hadn't even thought to ask!) We scheduled a taping session right then, and I began working on the outline and script for the tapes.

Only a few days later, I was making follow-up phone calls to the participants of a recent "Design Your Life" workshop I had conducted.

One of those phone calls was to Gene Tognacci. During the conversation, I asked Gene about his business and he began to explain to me about his work in broadcasting and communications. I mentioned to him that Sandy and I were scheduled to record a series of audiotapes on power networking, and he responded with some valuable ideas and offered his assistance. Within a few days, we had arranged for Gene to work with us on our tapes.

Having Gene produce the tapes for us was a blessing. He met with us to preview our script, sat in on our taping sessions, edited the tapes, and helped to arrange and coordinate the process of duplicating and ordering the tapes, labels, cases, and other supplies.

This was a project that was new to us and could have been long and laborious. Instead, with Gene and Tess's assistance we were able to move quickly, enjoy the experience, and learn a great deal. Every time there was a decision to make, we had someone to turn to for advice. We became a team that was focused on the success of the project, cheering each other on and developing a friendship that has grown since then.

A long-time friend and a new friend made the difference in having our dream come true. We were clear about the end product we wanted. Tess and Gene were able to direct and support us all along the way. It was great to accept their support and to experience the ease, joy, and fun of teamwork and accomplishment.

Tess and Gene both attended our "Power Networking" workshop, and we surprised them by calling them up to the front of the room, sharing the story about the tapes, acknowledging them for their support, and giving them the first two tape sets that were produced! It is true that working as a member of a team is more enjoyable and effective than working as a Lone Ranger!

PLAN YOUR ACTION;
ACT ON YOUR PLAN

1 Write a list of the values and principles that are important to you. (Write quickly as the words come to mind, without judging or evaluating.) After you have made your list, prioritize the items according to the following three categories:

1. What makes life meaningful for me

2. Important yet not a number-one priority

3. Nice to have

Remember that values are not right or wrong and that none are better than the others. Allow your instincts to guide you.

Reflect on your list once a day for three weeks. Reprioritize the list each day. At the end of the three weeks, review the list and notice which values were consistently prioritized as first. Take a clean sheet of paper and list your top values and principles. Post the list in your time management book, above your desk, or somewhere where you can review it on a regular basis.

. . . .

2 List your accomplishments in life, considering everything, including career, family and relationship, health and well-being, education, finance, personal development and spirituality, and hobbies and recreation. Review the list and highlight the accomplishments that are the most meaningful for you personally. Share with someone in your network what you identified as your most meaningful accomplishments.

. . . .

3 List your strengths and skills and review them along with your list of accomplishments in order to define how you want to be used as a resource for others. Identify at least one person you can contact to offer your support, and call that person right away!

4   Think of a project or goal that you have approached with the Lone Ranger mentality. Compose a letter telling people what your project or goal is and let them know how they can specifically support you. Make sure that the letter includes the following five components:

1. Acknowledge them for who they are for you and what they have done for you.

2. Be specific about what your project or goal is and what this project means for you and your business.

3. Be specific regarding what they can do to help you accomplish your goal.

4. Give them a definite and easy way to respond.

5. Let them know that you are available to support them.

Send the letter to at least twenty people in your network.

. . . .

5   Statistics indicate that most people have at least 250 contacts. Think of yourself as a resource (rather than as a separate, individual entity) connected with 250 other resources, each of whom is connected to 250 resources, and so on.

Visualization: Imagine 250 barely visible circuits that link you to over 250 people who also have circuits connecting them with others. Notice that no matter how far you follow the circuits, there is no end in sight. Imagine that even though the circuits are barely visible, you can reach out and touch them. Notice how strong the connections are; as you look closer, you can also see that each circuit is an open channel of energy that flows in both directions. Now notice that there is a light switch in your hand; you realize that all you need to do is flip on the switch to send a flow of energy that illuminates all the connections and circuits. Now flip the light switch and feel the power surge of energy that flows through you, out to your connections, and back to you!

6   Take several clean sheets of paper and list all of the goals that you want to accomplish personally and professionally. After you have completed your list, ask yourself the following four questions regarding each goal:

1. Am I willing to do what it takes to accomplish this goal?

2. Am I willing to be who I would have to be to accomplish this goal?

3. Am I willing to give up or change whatever has been in the way of my accomplishing this goal?

4. Is my motive for wanting to accomplish this goal in alignment with my top values and principles?

Whenever you answer yes to all four questions, highlight that goal. Once you have reviewed the whole list this way, mark beside each highlighted goal either "one month," "one year," "three years," "eight years," or "over twelve years." Then take a clean sheet of paper, write "This Month's Goals" at the top, and list your one-month goals. Take another clean sheet for your one-year goals, another for your three-year goals, and so on.

. . . .

7   Draw your network diagram. Take a blank sheet of paper and make a small circle in the middle with the word "YOU" in the circle. Think of the spheres of influence in your life and draw a spoke out from the circle with the name of each sphere of influence, such as "family," "church," "alumni association," "breakfast club," "civic club," or "professional association." From each major spoke draw branches with the names of the key people with whom you have relationships within each sphere of influence. Draw new branches from those people showing the connection they have to other contacts.

12

THE MIDAS TOUCH:
BE GRACIOUS AND COURTEOUS AS YOU NETWORK

---

8 **HAVE YOUR PRESENTATION PROFESSIONALLY REPRESENT WHO YOU ARE AND WHAT YOU DO.**

> **66** *The image you project, in many circumstances, is far more valuable than your skills or your record of past accomplishments.* **99**
>
> **Michael Korda**
> **As quoted in Og Mandino,**
>   ***Og Mandino's University of Success***

If you want to be perceived as a professional, then be sure to portray professionalism through your actions and presentation. Have your presentation, including your clothes, speech, and mannerisms, represent you in the best possible way as a statement of who you are and what you do.

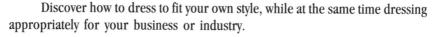

Discover how to dress to fit your own style, while at the same time dressing appropriately for your business or industry.

❏ Build a wardrobe that will serve you for all types of functions. Buy good-quality items that represent your own level of professionalism while providing the best wear and appearance for your money. It is better to have a few good outfits than many outfits of inferior quality.

❏ Learn how to accessorize and pull an outfit together beautifully.

❏ Be well groomed with shoes shined, nails clean and manicured, and hair styled.

❏ As a finishing touch, include a pleasant demeanor and natural smile.

If you are in doubt about what to wear for a specific business event, call and ask. It is better to risk being slightly overdressed rather than being under-dressed. Men can easily add or take off a tie or coat to be appropriately dressed for most situations. Women can include in their wardrobe outfits and accessories that are easy to adapt to various types of functions and events.

If you are in doubt about any aspect of your wardrobe or want to update your look, we recommend the services of a professional image consultant. With a good image consultant, you can develop a style and wardrobe that supports you personally and professionally.

If you use your vehicle in your business, keep it clean inside and out. When you transport a client or prospect, you do not want to have to apologize for how your car looks or runs. If you use a briefcase, be sure that it is well organized and attractive.

Another effective presentation tool is the use of a written agenda, prepared in advance, for your appointments and meetings. Clients and prospects will appreciate the way an agenda helps them to use their time effectively. This attention to detail also conveys respect, appreciation, and professionalism.

Representing yourself professionally will add polish and power to your networking. People will interact with you as a respected peer and will be more likely to send you powerful networking opportunities.

9 INTRODUCE YOURSELF IN A WAY THAT IS CLEAR, CONCISE, AND PERSONABLE, AND THAT GENERATES INTEREST.

> 66 *Making introductions, being introduced, and introducing yourself are a necessary part of effective networking in all situations—at network gatherings, business meetings, and social situations.* 99
>
> **Leslie Smith, Associate Director**
> **National Association of Female Executives**

You have probably heard about the importance of the first impression. For many people the first impression is the lasting one. Although you may get the opportunity to alter the first impression, the ideal situation is to make it strong and positive through the way you introduce yourself.

One of your greatest assets can be a self-introduction that develops relationship and rapport while generating interest. Although it usually takes only seven to ten seconds to introduce yourself, it is something you will have the opportunity to do many times throughout your life. When someone asks, "What do you do?" you want to be prepared to respond with something other than "I am a CPA" or "I am an attorney." These responses indicate who you are, not what you do. The important information to give people is what you do, what service you offer— what is *special* about who you are and what you do.

The way you introduce yourself can either turn people off, leave them cold, or draw them in. You want to capitalize on every opportunity you have to promote yourself and your business when you introduce yourself. Take the time to think about and develop your self-introduction with the following criteria as your guideline:

Criteria for a Powerful Self-Introduction

Clear   Be sure to let people know what you do. You want
                                 people to be intrigued but not confused.

Concise	Follow the KISS rule (Keep It Short and Simple). Develop an introduction that says what you want to say in seven to ten seconds. The "seven-second syndrome" indicates that the first impression happens in the first seven seconds of meeting someone.
Distinctive	Be catchy enough to distinguish yourself from everyone else while also being professional. You can do this by telling people through your introduction what you love about what you do, what your commitment is to your clients, or what is special about the way you do business.
Relatable	Use common words (rather than buzzwords or technical terms) and examples that people can relate to so that you immediately develop relationship and rapport.
Engaging	Your words, mannerisms, tone of voice, and eye contact can all contribute to people being intrigued, interested, and drawn to you. They will tend to remember your warmth, smile, interest, and enthusiasm.

Compare these two examples of self-introductions:

1. "Hi, I'm Donna Fisher, public speaker and seminar leader."

2. "Hello, my name is Donna Fisher, coleader of the 'Power Networking' workshop."

The first introduction is vague and bland. The second has more impact because it is specific, distinctive, relatable, and engaging. The second is more likely to attract people's attention, generate inquiry, and be remembered.

There are still other options:

3. "Hello, my name is Donna Fisher, owner of Discovery Seminars. I can teach you to network anywhere and everywhere with everyone you meet to get whatever you want!"

4. "Good morning, my name is Donna Fisher. I teach networking as a way to build your business and enhance your life."

Example 3 is more outrageous and must be presented with a high level of energy and confidence. You can see that example 4 is clear, concise, easy to say, and professional.

Notice your own thoughts or opinions regarding the various examples to learn what appeals most to your style and interests. You may want to create several versions for use in various situations and circumstances. It is important to gear the introduction to the group and to the message you want to convey.

Notice in the following examples how people have added an element of interest, warmth, and uniqueness to the second version of their introduction:

1. "Hello, my name is Lane Mabray, real estate agent."

2. "Hello, my name is Lane Mabray. I help people achieve the American dream, home ownership. I sell everything from condos to castles."

1. "Hello, my name is Ann Voss, optometrist."

2. "Hello, my name is Ann Voss and I help keep the world in focus. I am an optometrist."

1. "Hello, I'm Monte Pendleton, franchise consultant."

2. "Hello, I'm Monte Pendleton. I help small companies become large companies through franchising."

1. "Hello, I'm Gene Tognacci, producer of video programs."

2. "Hello, I'm Gene Tognacci. I produce sales and marketing video programs, from script to screen and everything in between."

1. "Hi, I'm Susie Davis. I own Just Desserts, a full-service catering business. We do corporate lunches to dinner parties and specialty baskets. We can work with your budget. We are located at . . ."

2. "Hi, I'm Susie Davis, owner of Just Desserts. But we cater more than *just desserts;* we want to work with you and your budget for a "tasty" presentation.

Develop your self-introduction until it is a natural expression of yourself that fits the situation. Practice different approaches until you find the words that best represent you while getting your message across so that people will remember you. Once you identify the words or phrases that best represent how you want to introduce yourself, you can adjust your introduction to fit each situation. Practice your introduction in front of the mirror until it is as natural and comfortable as saying your name.

Think about how many times you have the opportunity to introduce yourself to either an individual or a group of people. Think about how many times you are asked the question, "What do you do?" Your response can be simple, easy, and natural. At the same time, make sure that it generates interest, conveys your message, and has a positive, lasting effect.

10 BE AT EASE IN GROUPS AND USE CONVERSATION GENERATORS EFFECTIVELY.

> 66 *Too often we lose an opportunity to meet someone because we spend precious time trying to think of the perfect opening line.* 99
>
> Susan RoAne
> *How to Work a Room*

In a group or at a networking event, it may not be natural to formally introduce yourself by immediately giving your name and telling what you do. However, you *can* approach people with a simple statement or question that serves as an opener to conversation. Once you are in a conversation, you can ease into introducing who you are and what you do at the appropriate time.

The skill of generating conversation and rapport can be a great asset in networking situations. Conversation generators are icebreakers to which people can easily respond. Any comment, made either as a statement or a question, can provide the opportunity for others to engage in conversation with you. You can make a comment to someone on an elevator, on a plane, in a grocery store line, or at a networking event. Whether the conversation goes beyond the comment or not is irrelevant. You have done your part by graciously providing the opportunity for interaction.

A conversation generator generally relates to something you have in common with the other person. And you always will have something in common with any person—you are at the same event, work in the same office building, live in the same city, are shopping at the same store, and so on.

Conversation generator examples include:

"How did you get involved with the . . . Club?"

"What a beautiful facility for a banquet!"

"I hear the speaker for today is an expert on . . ."

"Can you tell me a little bit about this organization?"

"It looks as though we're going to have a full flight."

"This is my first time to attend a . . . meeting."

"Is this your first time here? Let me introduce you to . . ."

"Good morning, welcome to the . . ."

"I didn't realize there would be such a crowd."

"One of my clients told me that this seminar . . . !"

"I am looking for . . . Can you help me?"

Conversation generators are like offering your hand: easy to respond to, simple, and straightforward. You don't want to preach, teach, or put people on the spot. You do want to put people at ease.

Two keys to being confident when meeting people are *preparation* and *practice*. Plan your conversation generators so that you are comfortable approaching people. Practice with friends and in situations where you already feel comfortable, and you will soon be ready to branch out to new groups and situations. As meeting people becomes more natural and easier for you, you will be more effective at helping others feel at ease.

Your ability to be at ease in groups will enhance your enjoyment and effectiveness in social and business situations. By developing your social skills, you will develop greater confidence in your ability to meet people, generate conversation, and discover new networking opportunities.

11 REINTRODUCE YOURSELF TO PEOPLE RATHER THAN WAITING FOR THEM TO REMEMBER YOU.

> 66 *It is always a big person who walks up to you and offers his/her hand and says hello.* 99
>
> David J. Schwartz
> *The Magic of Thinking Big*

It is both courteous and professional to reintroduce yourself to someone you have met before. People will appreciate a reintroduction because it relieves them of the awkwardness of trying to recall who you are. Do not make other people guess or struggle to remember your name. Above all, do not say, "Do you remember me?" Your role as a networker is to support and empower others while putting them at ease.

When reintroducing yourself include, if possible, where you met the person or how you know him. This will reinitiate the relationship and establish rapport.

"The last time I saw you, you were doing a great job . . ."

"I know it has been a while, but I met you at . . . My name is . . . I was on the community action committee."

"My name is . . . and I believe I met you at . . ."

Do not act as if the other person *should* remember. Simply reintroduce yourself and use the current opportunity to further the relationship. By reintroducing yourself, you will reinforce your connection and it is likely that she will remember you from now on. You will also avoid any potential awkwardness, and your previous connection can serve as the common ground for conversation.

It is a great acknowledgment to be remembered, but do not take it as a slight when you are not. Use the opportunity to acknowledge the other person by remembering and relating to him appropriately.

12 FOCUS ON PEOPLE AS THEY ARE INTRODUCED TO YOU SO THAT YOU REMEMBER THEIR NAME AND WHO THEY ARE.

> **❝** *People don't always care how much you know, but they know how much you care by the way you listen.***❞**
> **Anonymous**

The key aspects of memory recall are *focus, association,* and *repetition.* You must be interested in people and realize the value of remembering them in order to be effective with memory recall. People like to be remembered and one of the highest compliments you can pay anyone is to listen and remember her name.

You can develop your ability to focus as you meet people so that name recollection is ensured. This requires that you give your full attention to each person. For example, rather than thinking ahead to what you are going to say next, focus on what the other person is saying. Be interested! This is why it is essential that you practice your self-introduction so that you can focus on who you are meeting rather than on what you are going to say.

To reinforce your ability to remember someone's name, associate it with something that you talked about, the event where you met, or the other person's occupation. You can use this technique not only to help you remember a name, but to help you remember what you want to recall about the person for future networking possibilities.

Engage in conversation with people, learn about them, relate to them, and develop rapport. Use their name in a natural way while talking with them. Every time you repeat their name, either to yourself, in conversation with them, or by introducing them to someone else, you are reinforcing their name and committing it to memory. Repetition can happen this way:

1. Hear the name as the person is introduced.

2. See the name as you glance at the person's nametag.

3. Say the name either during the conversation or as you are closing the conversation.

4. Look at the name once again when the person hands you his card.

5. Review your cards at the end of the day and once again notice the person's name and business.

6. Write the name in your organizer or your time management system for follow-up action.

Memory recall is essential to a networker because you must be able to remember people in order to respond to them and refer them to one another. The greater your ability to store and recall data, the more responsive you can be to the people in your network.

13 BECOME COMFORTABLE PLAYING HOST AT NETWORKING EVENTS.

66 Wherever there is a human being there is a chance for kindness.99
Seneca

The role of the host is to make people feel welcome, comfortable, and included at events. When you host your own party, you greet people, show them around, introduce them to others, and make sure that they have refreshments. You can play this role at any event that you attend and can enhance your own effectiveness while you are contributing to the success of the event.

There are several benefits of playing host:

You affect the success and flow of the event.

You are a catalyst that helps people interact with one another.

By introducing people to one another, you reinforce their names in your memory.

You help others to be at ease.

You experience more ease and comfort yourself.

When you are interacting in a group, notice when new people walk up, and invite them to join the conversation. As you introduce them, it is helpful, when possible, to say something about them that generates interest and conversation. For example:

"Joan, we've just been talking about . . . You probably have some interest in . . . as well, don't you?"

"Tom, let me introduce you to some people here."

"John, I'd like you to meet Gene. He helped us produce our audiocassette series."

Many people feel awkward at events and are uncomfortable meeting new people. If you happen to be one of these people, play host. Your own discomfort will disappear when you are taking care of others rather than being concerned about yourself. Without even thinking about it, you will notice that you are easily meeting and interacting with people.

14 BECOME COMFORTABLE PROMOTING AND CREATING VISIBILITY FOR YOURSELF AND YOUR BUSINESS.

> **66**Marketing can be a positive,
> exciting, ethical part of your business;
> you do not have to become a huckster
> to be a good marketer.**99**
>
> **Anthony O. Putman**
> *Marketing Your Services*

You are your own best public relations person. You are the one who knows best what you do and what you have to offer others. It is up to you to create visibility for yourself and use that visibility to promote yourself appropriately.

If you grew up hearing the phrase "Don't toot your own horn," you may feel uncomfortable promoting yourself. It is not necessary to be loud or boisterous to attract people's attention. You can promote yourself without appearing boastful or arrogant, but simply confident and professional. This is not about "tooting your own horn"—it is about not hiding your talents under a bushel basket!

It's okay to speak well of yourself; in fact, it's good to express confidence and a natural enthusiasm for your work. It's also important to let people know what you offer so that when they have a need you can fulfill they will call on you.

15 BE GRACIOUS AND COURTEOUS WITH EVERYONE YOU MEET.

❝Life is not so short but that there is always time enough for courtesy.❞

Ralph Waldo Emerson
Letters and Social Aims

Hectic lifestyles sometimes cause us to overlook common courtesy and good manners. Since networking is about people and relationships, it is important to make sure that the use of courtesy and good manners is a priority. There are many ways to be courteous:

❑ Be aware of the opportunity to hold a door or elevator for someone.

❑ When you are seated while being introduced to someone, rise and offer your hand in greeting.

❑ Assist others with their coats.

❑ Unlock and open your passenger's car door before your own.

❑ Ask how you can assist your host or hostess.

❑ RSVP promptly to invitations.

❑ Send a thank-you note after you attend an event.

You never know if someone you meet is going to be important in your life. Treat everyone with respect and courtesy so that people will enjoy and appreciate being around you. Being pleasant and cordial adds personal power and warmth to your networking.

NETWORKING —IN— ACTION

The Power of a Positive Self-Introduction–Michel Feray

A powerful, positive self-introduction helps you to be clear about what you have to offer to people and allows you to get your message across to people effectively. When you have your introduction "down pat," you can speak about who you are and what you do with a greater sense of confidence while focusing your attention on others.

This story from Michel Feray describes "how the power networking principles helped shape my career growth from being an employee of a printing service company to becoming owner-partner in my own creative studio." In one of our "Power Networking" workshops, during the section on "How to Make a Positive First Impression," Michel volunteered to have her introduction analyzed and revised.

She stood in front of the entire group and stated:

> Hello, my name is Michel Feray. I have been in the graphics industry for twenty years and I currently work for a company in the printing industry selling prepress color separations and printing services as well as freelancing as a photographer and graphic designer. This way I can turnkey jobs for clients. In other words, I can service a client's needs from an initial idea to designing a logo, producing an ad or brochure layout, taking commercial or portrait photographs, and handling the prepress and printing production. My job as a graphic media specialist is to service my clients' needs, whether by producing an advertisement, brochure, or photograph or creating a complete hardcover book, to help create a visual impression with graphic and photographic excellence and to service the production clear through to the printed page.

This was obviously longer than our recommended seven-second introduction and included what Michel later called "a paragraph of fumbling phrases and run-on ideas." Michel's many skills and services were lost because there was too much information for people to sort through to remember any one thing in particular. Michel eagerly and openly listened to feedback and ideas from the group and began to outline the key aspects that were important for developing a more concise statement.

She identified three important parts:

1. Who she was—Michel Feray

2. Her business or specialty—graphic media specialist

3. The distinctive value or interest she wanted to convey to the group—that she services a "diverse" clientele with graphic design and photography, from concept through to the printing process

With coaching and feedback, she moved through several versions to deliver an introduction to the group that attracted everyone's attention and interest:

> Hello, I'm Michel Feray. I specialize in *graphic media* and produce *turnkey projects* for a *diverse clientele* from initial *concept* through *design* and *photography* to the *printed page*.

Michel noticed that in the process of developing her introduction, she actually gained greater clarity and confidence about what she did and what she had to offer. Through the process of fine-tuning and repeating her introduction, she gained even more strength and power in her delivery.

The following week she was invited to a breakfast networking organization. Michel recounts:

> I was anxious to try out my new introduction techniques and imagined that I would be milling around casually in a group of people as we all convened for breakfast. When I arrived I found the breakfast club much more professionally organized than I had imagined. As the meeting began, each person stood up to introduce himself or herself to the group. I didn't know if I was really prepared for this audience, but the practice in the workshop helped me to stand up with confidence as my turn approached.

I did not know at the time that the group gave awards honoring the best introduction. At the end of the meeting the awards were announced. The Certificate of Recognition was read to the group: "This is to certify that Michel Feray gave an outstanding presentation . . . and is hereby honored for the best introduction giving a memorable, concise statement concerning her business, and has been so judged by a jury of peers at this meeting . . ." As I walked up to receive the certificate, I was told that it was very rare for a first-time guest to receive this honor!

With this type of feedback, Michel became even more confident and received more attention and referrals, which led to increased business. Five months later, as the results of Michel's networking continued to pay off, she and her partner started their own business, set up a new office, and developed together an established, reputable design and photography studio.

Michel wrote to us that "the introduction, confidence, and techniques I learned worked! And they have been working for me and my partner and our company with enormous success ever since. We have built the majority of our clientele in less than one year from networking, referrals, and offering creative excellence as graphic media specialists!"

Now this story may have had the same happy ending even without the powerful self-introduction; however, the momentum that was created appeared to move Michel along more quickly than she had ever expected. Don't underestimate the importance of your self-introduction. It is your opportunity to get people's attention and promote yourself and your business with a positive, powerful impact.

PLAN YOUR ACTION;
ACT ON YOUR PLAN

8 Clean out your closet, your car, and your office. Make a list of things to do or items to purchase that will align your presentation with the way you have defined your professional image.

. . . .

9 Write a self-introduction that fulfills the criteria in this section: It should be clear, concise, distinctive, relatable, and engaging. Practice saying your introduction out loud and make revisions as you practice. Review your ideas with a coach or mentor who will give you objective feedback. (Explain to the coach what you want to accomplish with your self-introduction.) Practice again in front of a mirror and experiment with phrasing, inflections, and tone of voice. You may even want to record the introductions on cassette and listen to them. Persist until you develop your self-introduction into a statement of who you are and what you have to offer that inspires you and draws others to you.

. . . .

10 Write out six conversation generators (statements and questions) that you would be comfortable saying to the new people you approach at meetings and events. Before you attend an event, review your list and revise your conversation generators to fit the particular occasion. After the event, make note of which statements and questions were most effective in generating the rapport and conversation that you desired.

11   Make a conscious decision to approach people whom you might not typically approach because you either have not seen them in a long time, only met them briefly, or fear that they will not remember you. Before you approach them, take a few seconds to recall who they are, where you met them, or how you know them. Think about what you will say as you reintroduce yourself, and then go ahead and take the initiative.

. . . .

12   Write an affirmation statement regarding your natural ability to remember and recall names and faces. Take a sheet of paper and make two columns. Write your affirmation in the left column and your mental response in the right column. Continue writing the affirmation followed by the response until the response is positive and in alignment with your affirmation. Do this daily for twenty-one days. For example:

Affirmation:	Mental Response:
I remember and recall names easily.	Oh yea? You forgot . . .
I remember and recall names easily.	Good idea, but . . .
I remember and recall names easily.	That would be nice.
I remember and recall names easily.	Maybe I could . . .
I remember and recall names easily.	I can do that!

This is just an example. It will typically take much more writing than this to get from negative responses to consistent, positive responses.

. . . .

13   Plan to attend a networking event and discreetly "play host." Think ahead about "your" event and all "your" guests. Place your total attention on playing host and write down your thoughts and observations afterward.

14
In front of a mirror in a room by yourself, practice promoting yourself with the following personas:

❏ Arrogant

❏ Shy

❏ Confident

❏ More arrogant

❏ More shy

❏ Totally confident

. . . .

15
Make your own list of "gracious and courteous behaviors."

CHAPTER

13

THE FIRST STEP–RAPPORT:
HANDLE BUSINESS CARDS
WITH RESPECT

16 CREATE BUSINESS CARDS THAT ARE ATTRACTIVE AND REPRESENTATIVE OF WHO YOU ARE AND WHAT YOU DO.

> **66** *The purpose of business cards is to give people a tangible, physical way to remember you.* **99**
>
> **Susan RoAne**
> *How to Work a Room*

Your business card is your "calling card." It represents you when you are not there and speaks for you and your business long after you have given it away. Make sure that your card is attractive, appealing, and easy to read, and that it conveys the message you want people to remember.

The importance of this one small piece of business communication warrants investing time and money in the talents of a good graphic designer. Ask for several ideas to choose from and carefully select the colors, design, lettering, and quality of paper. Also, make sure that your business card is compatible with the rest of the written materials that go out of your office.

Your card should be informational and descriptive of your business. Do not (1) include too much copy, (2) make the print too small, or (3) make it difficult to read or understand. Remember, the purpose of your card is to provide easy reference and recall of your name, business, address, and phone number.

Your "calling card" is you. It will be seen by many people, may be passed around to people who have not yet met you, and will serve as a reminder to others of who you are and what you do.

17 HAVE SUFFICIENT BUSINESS CARDS HANDY FOR EACH SITUATION.

❝ Taking the time to 'be prepared' can be the best investment you make. ❞

Susan RoAne
How to Work a Room

Always have more business cards than you think you might need and be organized so that your cards are handy and easily accessible. If you are attending an event, do your homework and find out how many people will be attending and what type of networking opportunities will be available.

Always keep your cards in the same place so you know where they are and can reach them easily. Do not mix them in with the cards that are handed to you; you should be able to access your card without having to search through a stack of assorted cards. The ideal system is to use one pocket for your cards, one pocket for cards you receive that require no immediate action, and another pocket for cards that require immediate or special follow-up. Also keep a pen handy for making notes on the cards you receive.

A little preparation can go a long way. Get in the habit of replenishing your supply of business cards when you return from an event and checking your supply before you leave for an event or meeting. By thinking ahead, you will have cards when you need them to respond to the people you meet.

18 GIVE OUT YOUR BUSINESS CARDS APPROPRIATELY.

> ❝ *The exchange of cards should*
> *follow a conversation in which rapport*
> *has been established.* ❞
>
> Susan RoAne
> *How to Work a Room*

Passing out business cards randomly and indiscriminately is not an effective use of your cards. Do not give them out just to have them be forgotten or tossed away. Develop the ability to discern quality contacts and make the exchange of cards in a way that will solidify these contacts.

An exchange of cards should be based on a rapport that has been established, an obvious business connection, or a follow-up action that has been identified. Remember, these are your calling cards and you want to share them with people whom you want in your network. When you treat the act of giving someone your business card with respect, the recipient will also tend to treat the card, interaction, and follow-up with respect.

Your business cards should be used when you give a lead or referral to someone. As you refer that person to someone else in your network, make a note on the back of your card with the name and phone number of the contact and information on what the contact does.

Although every event is an opportunity for networking, do not become a "networking mongrel" (see Chapter Two). Networking mongrels are so focused on their own agenda that they intrude, gather cards without connecting with people, abuse social events for business purposes, and forget to offer support or appreciation for others.

Act appropriately for the event and the situation. At social events, make sure that your primary attention is on the purpose of the event. If an important opportunity presents itself, be discreet in exchanging cards and making plans for a business follow-up.

19 MAKE NOTATIONS ON BUSINESS CARDS THAT YOU RECEIVE AS MEMORY JOGGERS AND FOLLOW-UP REMINDERS.

66People don't care about how much you know until they know how much you care.99

Harvey B. Mackay
Swim with the Sharks Without Being Eaten Alive

Business cards are a tool that allows you to easily recall and contact people. It is recommended that you make notations on business cards once you have had an interaction with a person. These notes can include any of the following data:

The date

The meeting or event

The highlight of the conversation

The circumstance of the meeting

Who introduced you

Any interesting information about the person

The follow-up action that has been identified

This assists you in following up efficiently and remembering the person for future contact. The more you know about someone, the more likely you are to remember that person and thus refer to her or call on her.

Make the notes on the business card as soon as it is appropriate. This may be when you have finished your conversation and can take a quick moment by yourself to jot items down. Or it may be as soon as you are back at your car or your office, while your conversation is fresh in your mind. It is appropriate to jot down a note on the card while you are with the person if you are setting up a follow-up appointment or designating some action to take. This will let him know that you plan to follow up on the conversation.

Always review your business cards right away, make any follow-up notes in your time management system, and feed them into your filing system. By doing this you will ensure that the information will not get lost while at the same time you will reinforce the information in your own memory bank.

NETWORKING
—IN—
ACTION

A Chance Encounter Leads to Major Results–Sandy Vilas

I arrived at a local hotel one-half hour prior to a presentation I was delivering to a luncheon networking club. One of the members, Jack Fallas, came over to introduce himself to me and expressed disappointment that he would miss the presentation because he had just received a phone call regarding a meeting he had to attend.

Although our conversation was brief, we sensed that it would be good to talk further and I agreed to call Jack when I got back to my office. We exchanged cards and I wrote a note on the back of the card he handed me as a reminder to call him. I then slipped the card into the inside pocket of my jacket and went on to give my presentation. (I use that pocket for cards I receive that I know I want to follow up on immediately. I use one coat pocket for my own cards and the other for cards I collect that require no immediate action.)

After the luncheon, I returned to my office, pulled out the card, and made the phone call. Rapport was established immediately, we got to know each other better, and we talked about Jack's role as a financial planner with a large brokerage firm headquartered in New Jersey. Jack referred me to the president of his firm and, based on Jack's recommendation, our firm had a selling agreement with them within two weeks. This firm was the largest brokerage firm that our company did business with that year and our business with them represented a significant portion of my income and our firm's success.

You never know what opportunities and relationships are available through "chance" networking encounters. Use your business cards as a tool for developing rapport and ensuring prompt follow-up. They are your "calling cards." Don't leave your office without them.

PLAN YOUR ACTION:
ACT ON YOUR PLAN

16 Hold your business card in your hand and answer the following questions:

❑ Is it attractive and appealing?

❑ Does it clearly represent who I am and what I offer?

❑ Does it include all the information people would need to contact me?

❑ Is all the information correct and easy to read?

❑ Is it the quality that I want?

❑ Is it a card that I am pleased to hand out to people?

❑ Is there anything I would like to change about the card?

Take whatever action is appropriate based on your answers to these questions.

. . . .

17 Check your supply of business cards and reorder if necessary (after you have reevaluated your card as indicated in number 16). Place a supply of business cards in your daily planner, briefcase, and/or purse. Place a backup supply of cards in the glove compartment of your car. To make sure that the cards stay clean, put your backup supply in a plastic bag.

. . . .

18 For two weeks, play a game with yourself regarding the handing out of business cards. The parameters of the game are that you can only give people your card (1) if they ask for it, (2) if you give them a referral, or (3) if you are offering support and need to let them know how to contact you.

19 Before the close of your business day, review the business cards you have received and mark the date in the upper right-hand corner. Also write, on either the front or the back of the card, where you met, follow-up action, interests identified, who introduced you (if pertinent), and any other information that might be beneficial. If you make notes on the back of the card, it is helpful to write the word "over" in parentheses on the front so that you won't forget to look at the back.

CHAPTER
14

A THOUGHTFUL PERSON IS A REMEMBERED PERSON:
NURTURE YOUR NETWORK WITH ACKNOWLEDGMENTS

20 RECEIVE AND GIVE ACKNOWLEDGMENTS DAILY

> **66** *The people who are successful are those who are grateful for everything they have.* **99**
>
> **Alan Cohen**
> *The Dragon Doesn't Live Here Anymore*

Acknowledgment is the act of giving positive feedback to another person. It is a simple and yet powerful tool because it reinforces and gives attention to what is being acknowledged. Acknowledgment is more than giving people compliments—it empowers them by providing authentic, constructive feedback.

Imagine turning up your own awareness and consciousness regarding what is going on around you. Begin to notice people, what they are doing, and how they are contributing. Do not assume that people know they are appreciated. For example, if you see someone being helpful, doing a good job, or being a responsive networker, acknowledge that fact. If you experience benefit from a referral, let the other person know that the referral was valuable. You can never overacknowledge as long as your acknowledgment is sincere, comes from the heart, and is given as a gift.

There is great power in giving and receiving acknowledgment. Because it is a form of sharing, it requires a certain amount of vulnerability. This vulnerability will enhance and deepen the amount of trust and respect in your networking relationships and make them more powerful.

Acknowledge authentically, spontaneously, and generously while expecting nothing in return. You can be a role model and a catalyst for acknowledgment throughout your network.

21 ACKNOWLEDGE THE PEOPLE WHO INSPIRE YOU WHETHER OR NOT YOU PERSONALLY KNOW THEM.

66 *It takes bigness of spirit to praise the great and the successful instead of envying them.* **99**

David Dunn
Try Giving Yourself Away

Inspiration can come from someone you know, something you read, or something you observe. In any case, whether your inspiration comes from a long-time friend, a passing acquaintance, a famous person, or a community leader, always remember to acknowledge those who inspire you.

The list of possible categories of people who may inspire you is virtually endless:

Authors	Co-workers	Family
Business people	Educators	Friends
Children	Employees	Spouse
Community leaders	Employers	Volunteers

Do not assume that people already receive a lot of praise and positive reinforcement. Most people mean well but tend to forget to pass along those words of praise or encouragement. Remember how good you feel when your contributions are noticed and appreciated. Let that be your focus and reminder to praise and acknowledge others for the inspiration, role model, or contribution that they provide for you.

22 NURTURE YOUR NETWORK WITH CALLS, NOTES, AND GIFTS IN A TIMELY AND APPROPRIATE MANNER.

❝ *He who praises another enriches himself far more than he does the one praised. To praise is an investment in happiness.* **❞**

David Dunn
Try Giving Yourself Away

The word *nurture* means to promote growth and development. You can nurture your network so that it grows and develops into a powerful entity of contacts and supportive relationships. If there were such a thing as a network meter, its gauge would be based on the quality of the network's relationships. And relationships grow and develop best when they are given time, energy, and caring attention.

Staying in touch with people will keep your network alive and well. This can easily be done in the form of notes, cards, calls, gifts, and visits. Develop the habit of nurturing your networking in the following ways:

❑ Every week, call at least one person whom you have not talked to in at least ninety days. This implements an ongoing process of reactivating your "hidden network."

❑ Send a gift or note as soon as possible when another person has served or supported you in some way.

❑ Invite people in your network to events that you are participating in when you know that the event would be of interest or value to them.

❑ Send clippings and articles from papers or magazines. When someone you know is in the paper, send her a copy of the article and a congratulatory note. When you see an article that relates to someone's business, industry, or personal projects, send it to him along with a short note.

Here are some additional ideas on how to develop the habit of sending notes regularly:

❑ Keep your notecards handy.

❑ Designate a certain time in your schedule to write notes to people.

❑ Use the time you spend on airplanes or commuting to work (if you are not driving yourself) or any other free time during your day to catch up on your thank-you notes.

❑ Whenever you think of someone to whom you want to write a note, either do it right then or add it to your "to do" list.

❑ Place a certain number of notecards in your briefcase at the first of each week and make sure that they have all been written before you replenish your supply for the next week.

Here are some ways to begin your notes:

"Thank you for . . ."

"I appreciated . . ."

"It was great to . . ."

"Your support yesterday . . ."

"I enjoyed reading about you (your company) in . . ."

"Congratulations on your recent . . ."

The effect of notes is much greater than many people realize. The note actually reinforces the contribution while giving the sender the opportunity to express her appreciation. It is through the writing of the note that the full impact of the contribution comes alive for both parties.

As you nurture your relationships with cards, notes, and gifts, your network will grow and thrive. Just as any living organism must be fed and taken care of, your network will be taken care of by the regularity of your contacts, referrals, acknowledgments, and participation.

23 USE PERSONALIZED NOTECARDS.

66 *The handwritten note . . . reflects personal care, thought, and time expended.* **99**

Susan RoAne
How to Work a Room

As a networker, you will have many opportunities to send notes to the people in your network. Notecards designed specifically for you and your business give a very professional and successful image to your correspondence. Personalized notecards give you an easy, convenient way to communicate with people while sending a visual reminder of you and your company.

Although the computer has made it easier to send form letters and respond to the masses, the handwritten note continues to be a valued and respected form of communication. Over 60 percent of the people who responded to a survey conducted by the A. T. Cross Company indicated that they wished they took time to send more notes. Even though we have greater and faster means of communication today, the personal note is still viewed as the most thoughtful and meaningful method of saying thanks. A handwritten note provides a personal touch that represents care, thoughtfulness, and sincerity.

Give yourself the stature, credence, and professional spark that personalized notecards will add to your correspondence. You will find yourself eager and proud to send notes to your clients, associates, and fellow networkers.

24 GRACIOUSLY RECEIVE AND ACCEPT ACKNOWLEDGMENT AND SUPPORT.

> 66 *There is nothing that more obviously separates the powerful from the powerless than graciousness.*99
>
> Sherry Suib Cohen
> *Tender Power*

Some people tend to dismiss and deflect acknowledgment by saying, "Oh, that was nothing." If you think about it, this type of response can actually be disrespectful to the giver, the acknowledgment, and the receiver. Someone is giving you an opinion in the form of feedback, praise, or encouragement, and the least you can do is accept the opinion graciously, honoring that what the person is saying is true for him. You can even consider the possibility that what is being said is *true* and simply something you have not been able to see because of your own judgments and expectations of yourself. If you do not accept acknowledgment, you are probably enmeshed in negative thoughts of "If only I had . . . ," "I should have . . . ," "I wish I had . . . ," and you will miss the acknowledgment, satisfaction, and celebration of your own accomplishments.

When you receive support, be appreciative of the gift. It is a very high compliment and honor for people to want to support you and it is a compliment to accept the support they offer. As a power networker, you will realize that accepting the support of others is the smart way to accomplish what you want with the greatest ease, enjoyment, and success.

"Thank you" is always an appropriate response when someone acknowledges you or offers support. Develop your ability to receive and accept acknowledgment and support with graciousness and humility: you will discover the richness of your network.

Special Delivery to the First Lady— Donna Fisher

For over seven years, I specialized in working with volunteer programs and the nonprofit sector. I have a special love for promoting and supporting volunteerism and give a presentation on "Volunteerism: The Backbone of Our Country" to organizations throughout the community.

During all of the publicity about the "Thousand Points of Light" program and the attention the White House gave to promoting volunteerism early in the Bush administration, I decided to write First Lady Barbara Bush. I wanted to let her know how much I appreciated the renewed attention and "good press" that volunteerism was getting through her endeavors. I also wanted to express my appreciation to her for being a gracious role model for others, and I wished to offer my services to support any of her volunteer endeavors in Houston.

Well, I wrote and rewrote my letter. Once I was ready to mail it, I began to think about the concept that anyone is only four to five contacts away. I wondered whether I should just address it to First Lady Barbara Bush, White House, Washington, D.C., or if there might be a better way to have it delivered. After I brainstormed with Sandy about the possibility, he said that he wanted to check on something. He remembered a college friend, Jim Pierce, who was related to the Bush family in some way. Sandy called, reconnected with Jim, and explained the situation, and Jim immediately offered to take the letter to his aunt (Barbara Bush), whom he was planning to see that coming weekend. By that afternoon the letter was in Jim's hand, and I was pleased to know that this letter of acknowledgment, appreciation, and offer of support would be personally placed in Mrs. Bush's hands.

It would have been easy to simply place the letter in the mail, not let anyone know that I was writing to the First Lady, and send it with the attitude: "Que será será." It was great to get a letter back from the White House, but whether I had gotten a response or not, the experience of writing and sending the letter would have been satisfying in itself. This story is a reminder to me to express my appreciation of others (no matter who they are), utilize the resources around me, and not have my preconceived notions or ideas get in the way of pursuing every possible route to fulfillment.

Statistics indicate that anyone we want to meet, contact, or have a conversation with is only four to five steps away. This concept, called "global stepping-stones," is your avenue for connecting with people everywhere. Do you ever think, "What if I could make contact with . . . ?" or "Wouldn't it be great if I ran into . . . ?" or "If only I could reach . . ." The concept of global stepping-stones can be your reminder of how available people are. With the wise and resourceful use of your network, you can contact people who may have previously seemed out of your reach.

The Power of Acknowledgment– Estelle Murray

Estelle Murray is a bright, energetic woman who attended our workshop and was eager, receptive, and responsive throughout the day. Although she already very effectively used the principles of networking, she seemed to be reenergized and inspired. She was especially excited about the idea of giving positive feedback and acknowledgments to the people all around her.

Being in the placement business, Estelle always noticed what other placement firms were doing, and she was particularly impressed with a brochure that she saw from a competitor's company. Spurred on by her renewed vigor for acknowledgment, she called the partner of the firm and conveyed her praise for the firm's excellent promotional literature. She and the partner hit it off and scheduled a lunch the following week. Their conversation over lunch uncovered common interests and led to an offer to Estelle to be partner and president of the firm. Estelle accepted the offer and after three weeks at the firm she called us to schedule a networking training for her new staff.

We conducted a full-day training with the staff on "How to Utilize Networking as an Effective Marketing Tool." During that day, Estelle shared with us this story about how an acknowledgment to someone she did not even know had led to an exciting opportunity for her. We felt that this would be a great story to share regarding the power of giving acknowledgment, expecting nothing in return, and operating with an open mind. We acknowledge Estelle for her enthusiasm, support, loving energy, and commitment to the people around her.

PLAN YOUR ACTION: ACT ON YOUR PLAN

20 Think of five people you can acknowledge and write their names (one per day) with the abbreviation "TY" (thank you) beside their name in your time management system. Then write "TY" in your time management system for each of the next twenty-five days. Every day, either call or mail a note to the person listed and highlight her name to indicate that the acknowledgment was communicated. As you think of other people to acknowledge, write their names beside the abbreviation "TY" on one of the remaining days.

. . . .

21 At least once a month include in your acknowledgments someone you do not know personally. Which people in your industry, church, community, or professional association do you admire or appreciate? Send them a note of acknowledgment!

. . . .

22 Thought to remember: "A thoughtful person is a remembered person."

. . . .

23 If you already have personalized notecards and you are pleased with them, make sure that you are well stocked for your new focus on daily acknowledgment. If your supply is low, reorder them. If you do not have notecards or are not pleased with what you have, call your graphic designer and schedule an appointment. Decide whether you want postcards or fold-over notecards. Do you want envelopes printed too, or do you want the notes to fit into your standard stationery envelopes? Review design ideas, size, color, and printing options with your designer so that you will have a finished product that you are pleased with and that you will enjoy sending to people.

. . . .

24   A simple thank-you is often the most gracious response when someone acknowledges you or gives you a compliment. Practice saying "thank you."

MAXIMIZE YOUR ACTIONS:
MANAGE YOURSELF AS A RESOURCE

25 **ESTABLISH AN EFFECTIVE SYSTEM FOR ORGANIZING AND RETRIEVING YOUR NETWORK.**

> **❝***I work as hard as anyone, and yet I get so little done. I'd do so much you'd be surprised, if I could just get organized!***❞**
>
> **Douglas Malloch**

For every networker the one thing that can be his greatest asset or biggest nightmare is his system for organizing and retrieving the names, addresses, phone numbers, and other information about the people in his network. There are many ways to set up your filing system. The best approach is to develop a system that suits you, that is easy for you to keep up to date, and that provides easy access to names and numbers.

Systems to consider include:

1. A *business card file or Rolodex system,* where business cards are filed alphabetically by either last name or business. In some situations people collect two cards in order to file one under each listing.

2. An *index card system,* where all pertinent data are recorded on an index card. The cards can be organized by last name, business name, industry, event, or any other category you choose.

3. A *spiral notebook system,* where a notebook is used to record all interactions and provide a chronological record that includes the name, date, event, results of each contact, and other pertinent information from the conversation.

4. A *computer database management system,* where all data are entered into the computer with codes for industries, organizations, events and clubs, and follow-up information with dates. This provides many sorting, listing, and mailing capabilities.

There are no right or wrong systems, only systems that do or do not work for you personally. Knowing what you know about yourself and your activities, what type of system would you be most likely to keep up with and use? Take a look at all aspects of how you operate, what would serve you, what your objectives are, and what would be easiest for you to keep up to date. For example, do you enjoy computers or do you tend to shy away from them? Are you always out making calls, and do you need to have names and numbers in your briefcase and at your fingertips? Do business cards provide the most effective reference system to help you recall people?

Devise a system that keeps you organized and effective in building, retrieving, and working your network. Remember that the main objective is accessibility. If you can't find information, you can't refer to it, share it, or distribute it. Be organized so that you can remember people, find their information, and respond in a timely and proficient manner.

26 MY BUSINESS CARD FILE IS ORGANIZED AND UP TO DATE.

66 The most important word in the English language, if you want to be a success, can't be found in the dictionary. It's 'Rolodex.' 99

Harvey B. Mackay
Swim with the Sharks Without Being Eaten Alive

Keeping your business card file and follow-up system organized and up to date is a critical aspect of networking effectiveness. Develop a habit of feeding information into your system promptly so that you will be able to utilize the system efficiently.

Whatever system you devise for yourself, make a commitment to follow it for at least six months. After six months, review how well it is working and make any changes that would improve it. Also, schedule yourself to redo your file or list at least once or twice a year. The first of the year is an ideal time to review the list, weed out old information, and generate up-to-date, fresh records to start off your year.

Remember to make a note when you learn that someone has moved or changed jobs. Do not let cards sit in your coat pocket for weeks or get lost on your desk. Develop the habit of feeding data into your system on a daily or weekly basis. When you update the information in your system right away, you will always be working with current and accurate data.

27 USE A TIME MANAGEMENT SYSTEM EFFECTIVELY.

> **❝** *Time passes at a predetermined*
> *rate no matter what we do. It is a*
> *question not of managing the clock but*
> *of managing ourselves in respect to the*
> *clock . . . the heart of time manage-*
> *ment is management of self.* **❞**
>
> **Alec R. Mackenzie**
> *The Time Trap: Managing Your Way Out*

You do not have to be at the mercy of a busy schedule. However, when you have a busy schedule, it is especially important to use your time wisely and manage yourself well. Schedule your time and manage yourself to maximize opportunities and create balance and fulfillment in all areas of your life.

A time management system can be a useful tool to ensure that you are efficient and effective in accomplishing the day-to-day tasks that will help you reach your goals. A daily schedule allows you to outline your calls and appointments. A "to do" list can assist you in getting things accomplished in an orderly and timely fashion.

Make your time management system your friend and ally. Do not be a slave to a time management system, but do use a system that supports you in being well organized and productive. By using it properly, you will not have to worry about items falling through the cracks. You will achieve results and complete tasks with ease and efficiency.

Most time management systems include sections for goals, projects, prospects, addresses and phone numbers, expenses, delegation items, meeting notes, and an annual calendar. Pick the sections that apply to your business and personal activities and use them. Do not allow your system to be another source of clutter but rather a clearinghouse that supports your effectiveness.

Develop a natural attitude of respect for your own time and you will find that others will respect it as well. Stop saying that you don't have enough time. Manage your time wisely and have it be your greatest ally. Control where and how you spend your time. You will experience better organization and greater efficiency, which will provide better control and utilization of your resources.

28 COMPLETE YOUR DAILY ACTION LIST EACH DAY BY TRANSFERRING OR CHECKING OFF ITEMS.

> 66 *The way you ensure that you keep moving towards your goals and objectives . . . is to keep a daily 'to do' list.* 99
>
> **Marlene Wilson**
> *Survival Skills for Managers*

One key to efficient time management and organization is to plan your work for each day and then work your plan. List things to do and people to call in your daily planner and when each item is completed, either highlight it or check it off. Make a note immediately regarding the next step or follow-up action. At the end of the day, transfer tasks that were not accomplished to the appropriate future date. Having a plan for your day will help you to accomplish the daily tasks that support your networking endeavors and result in fulfillment of your personal and professional goals.

Small accomplishments and results lead to greater achievements, one day at a time. Keep your long-range objectives in mind as you go through your day and you will have the incentive to handle the daily tasks that can further your overall plan.

Completion creates freedom, clarity, and efficiency. Get rid of any clutter in your life. Stop nagging yourself with the thought that "there's too much to do" or "I don't have enough time." The habit of working your action list, completing each day, and planning the next day will enhance your power and effectiveness.

29 DO WHAT IS IN FRONT OF YOU RATHER THAN CREATING MORE ITEMS ON YOUR ACTION LIST.

> **❝***Managing your time isn't the real issue. Your time is fixed. What you need is to manage the activities that are consuming your time.***❞**
>
> **Kenneth Blanchard and Norman Vincent Peale**
> *The Power of Ethical Management*

Your daily planner will have a list of action items that you would like to complete each day. While you are working on these items, other things will come along that require your attention. Develop the focus and discipline to accomplish items efficiently so that you are not adding more items to your list than you can regularly complete.

Let's say that you are talking on the phone to a person who wants you to mail her some literature. While you are on the phone, you can write the address on the envelope as she gives it to you. Then, as soon as you get off the phone, you can get the literature, put it in the envelope, add postage, and send it on its way. The item is handled and out of your way. If, instead, you write yourself a note to send this person the literature, you will have added to your list and later you will have to take even more time to get the envelope, look up the address, and find the literature. A very simple item can be a major ordeal or a quick, simple task. It is up to you!

This principle can be used in many situations. For example, rather than saying, "Let's get together sometime," go ahead and schedule a time to meet. Or when you think of a lead for someone, pull out your business card right then, write the information on the back of the card, and hand it to him.

Handling mail, memos, and paperwork is a primary arena for distractions and procrastination. Be clear about the options for paperwork:

❑ Take action

❑ Read

❑ File

❑ Delegate

❑ Initial and pass on

❑ Trash

Procrastination will allow tasks to snowball, making it more likely that items will be lost or forgotten. Do not create busywork for yourself. Learn to handle calls, mail, memos, and situations once and with completion.

30 RETURN PHONE CALLS WITHIN TWENTY-FOUR HOURS.

66*Procrastination limits the effective-ness of every human being. How much more all of us would accomplish if we did not wait until tomorrow!*99

Robert E. Megill
May I Touch Your Life?

Returning phone calls promptly is good business etiquette. It is not only courteous but an effective and efficient way to network and conduct business. Besides, a phone call that is not returned promptly could be a missed opportunity.

See if you can consistently return all phone calls before you leave the office at the end of the day. If this is not possible, think about setting up a support system to return phone calls more promptly.

When you return from lunch, vacation, or a trip out of town, review all of the phone calls and prioritize them in terms of importance. Mark each phone slip "A," "B," or "C"; put the slips in that order; and return the calls based on their priority. When you are out of the office (on business or pleasure) make sure that the person answering your phone tells people when you are scheduled to return. Often, when you are out of town on business, you can still call in and handle the calls promptly, which will relieve you of the dilemma of returning to a desk full of messages.

Returning phone calls within twenty-four hours is an excellent habit and discipline to develop. It is a habit that supports the flow of information throughout your network in a timely manner.

31 ORGANIZE YOUR THOUGHTS BEFORE MAKING A PHONE CALL TO REFERRALS, LEADS, OR PEOPLE IN YOUR NETWORK.

> 66 *There are four steps to accomplishment: plan purposefully, prepare prayerfully, proceed positively, and pursue persistently.* 99
>
> **Anonymous**

Before you make a call, organize your thoughts, define your purpose, and determine the results that you would like to achieve. If you will be making a request, think about how you can ask for what you want clearly and concisely. Determine the best approach given what you know about the person you are calling and her resources.

The following outline identifies the steps to think about as you prepare for a call:

1. Identify yourself.

2. Tell the other person who referred you.

3. State the purpose of your call.

4. Ask for permission and time for a conversation.

5. Gather information.

6. Identify the action or next step to take.

7. Summarize the call.

8. Offer your assistance.

9. Thank the other person for his time and support.

These steps are included in the following example:

Tom: "Hi, my name is Tom Wilson and Joan Smith recommended that I contact you about . . ."

Paula:	"Oh great, how do you know Joan?"
Tom:	"Joan and I have been working together on . . . and that is why she recommended I call you. She indicated that you . . . Do you have a minute to talk about this with me?"
Paula:	"Sure, what are you looking for?"
Tom:	"I am looking for . . ."
Paula:	"What I recommend is . . ."
Tom:	"Thanks, that's very helpful. I will . . . How can I support you?"
Paula:	"Thanks, but I'm doing fine."
Tom:	"Well, here's an idea for you. What about . . . ?"
Paula:	"Hey, that's a good idea. Thanks, I will follow up on that."
Tom:	"Thanks very much for your time and assistance. Have a great day!"

When you organize your thoughts before you call, you will not only be more effective; you will be appreciated for being purposeful, powerful, and respectful of the other person's time.

32 SAY NO TO EVENTS, ACTIVITIES, AND MEETINGS THAT DRAIN YOUR TIME, ENERGY, OR FOCUS.

*66 If you are to do what you want
with your time, you must learn not to
do what you don't want.99*
Anonymous

Choose wisely the events, activities, and meetings in which you plan to participate. As a powerful networker, you will be invited to participate in many functions and projects. You must be respectful of your own time, energy, and focus. Do not allow yourself to be pulled in too many directions. Be sure to consider all the ramifications and motives of your participation and how it will best serve you and your network.

In terms of networking events, check to see if the time, purpose, and audience is a fit for you. Review the following information before you make your reservation:

What type of event is it?

Who is sponsoring the event?

What is the purpose of the event?

What are the date, time, duration, and location of the event?

Who are the known and probable attendees?

What are the potential benefits for you and your network?

How probable is it that you will attain those benefits?

This type of review will assist you in choosing events that will be a worthwhile use of your time and energy. Do not get caught in the game of trying to be all things to all people. You must take care of yourself in order to be available to others; otherwise, you will slowly lose your momentum and become ineffective with the people around you.

33 PREPARE FOR NETWORKING EVENTS IN ORDER TO MAXIMIZE YOUR OPPORTUNITY.

> **66** *The meeting of preparation with opportunity generates the offspring we call luck.* **99**
>
> **Anthony Robbins**
> *Unlimited Power*

Once you have done your research and decided to attend an event, take the time to prepare.

❏ Ask yourself what you want to accomplish on a personal and/or professional level.

❏ Prepare and practice a self-introduction that is geared to the event and your purpose.

❏ Identify several conversation generators that are suitable for the occasion and comfortable for you.

❏ Make sure that you have an ample supply of business cards available and plan a way to have them easily accessible.

Networking events can be very powerful tools in achieving your goals and expanding your network. It is easy to attend events, meet new people, and collect lots of cards; however, as a power networker you will do much more than that. You will develop your ability to always make solid contacts and establish valuable action items that will lead to new, exciting opportunities.

124

Responding Promptly Creates Opportunity–Sandy Vilas

Anne Boe and Bettie Youngs wrote the book *Is Your "Net" Working?* in 1989 and we happened to find it in a bookstore in San Francisco soon thereafter. After reading it, we shared the thought that it would be great to meet the authors but did nothing to pursue the idea at that time.

A few months later, on a national conference call, one of the participants commented that he was learning to use his business cards to promote himself. I jumped in and offered some tips and ideas on business card etiquette. At the end of our interaction, another person on the call, George Roman, asked me if I had read the book *Is Your "Net" Working?* When I said that I had, he immediately went on to tell me that Anne Boe was a client and good friend of his. He gave me her address and home phone number, adding that he had just talked to her that morning, and he recommended that I call her right away. As soon as the conference call was over, I dialed Anne's phone number.

We had a lengthy and enjoyable conversation, which resulted in the exchange of tapes and information on our networking activities. We had subsequent conversations after that and I sent her a draft of our book. It had all started through sharing information and ideas in a conference call; the boomerang came back, and I achieved a goal, made a new friend, and supported another person's networking efforts.

You never know what ideas or contacts may be available to you in a situation. In the simple process of doing what you do and serving others, you too will have opportunities "fall in your lap." Don't miss out when a lead, idea, or contact shows up right in front of you. Seize the opportunity to respond promptly and you will have networking miracles to share with your friends.

Networking Events Can Be Fun and Productive!–Dan Valdez

Networking events can be either a great opportunity or a drain on your schedule, time, and energy. With good organizational skills, wise choices, and a little preparation, you can learn to enjoy yourself and make valuable contacts when you attend networking events.

Dan Valdez went to networking events because they were "supposed" to be a great place to make business contacts. Although he did not enjoy attending these events and they never seemed to pay off in the way that he expected, he kept going because he thought he should.

Here is Dan's story in his own words:

> I have never really felt comfortable trying to get to know strangers, especially in a crowd where I hardly know anyone. I always felt somehow inadequate and unsure of myself. As a business owner, I knew I had to network and get to know new people, but I always hated it. I guess I had a fear of networking.
>
> My partner talked me into attending a "Power Networking" workshop, and I was amazed to discover that most of the people in the room felt exactly the way I did about networking events. I learned how to set goals for what I intended to accomplish at an event. I also discovered how to work my way into a conversation among strangers, how to use conversation generators effectively, and how to develop rapport when talking with people.
>
> Less than a week after the seminar, I attended a major annual networking event, as I do every year. I was eager to put some of my newly learned techniques to work and see how well I could do. I had a blast! I didn't want to leave after being there all day. The quality contacts I made turned into quality appointments. I had tremendous self-confidence while I was working the event, and the resulting relaxed attitude made the task enormous fun.
>
> Since the seminar, practicing the power networking techniques has turned from planned effort to instinct and habit. Knowledge of networking has furthered my career and company efforts far beyond anything I ever tried before.

Dan was determined to learn not only how to spend his time in a worthwhile way but how to have a good time as well. His willingness to learn and try new ideas created a dramatic shift from dreading events to enjoying them, from feeling uncomfortable to feeling confident and relaxed, and from collecting cards to making quality contacts.

Dan is now a very active member of a networking club and has been a powerful networking resource for many other people. He is a great role model for others on being efficient, gracious, confident, and effective in using networking as a lifestyle for success.

PLAN YOUR ACTION;
ACT ON YOUR PLAN

25 Place a list of the names and phone numbers of your immediate network in your time management planner. If you have a computer, establish or install a data base program that has efficient sorting, retrieving, and scheduling capabilities.

. . . .

26 Decide on the most effective means of organizing your business cards, for example, alphabetically by category, name, event, or company. Obtain a business card file box and file the cards in the order you have chosen. Review the cards as you are filing them and throw away any that do not mean anything to you.

. . . .

27 Carry with you a time management planner with a list of names and phone numbers, a schedule of your appointments, a list of calls to make and tasks to accomplish, and a place for making notes regarding new contacts.

. . . .

28 Check off or highlight each item on your daily schedule as you complete it. When you see that an item will not be completed, place a "T" for "transfer" beside it and transfer the item to another date.

29 Catch yourself when you start to say, "We ought to get together sometime!" and instead say, "I would like to schedule a time to get together with you." Pull out your time management planner, recommend a date and time, and you will have an appointment rather than just a good idea!

. . . .

30 Develop a reputation for being responsive by returning your phone calls. Let people know that they are important to you. Some possible openings are:

"Hi, I'm returning your phone call. What can I do for you?"

"Hello . . . , I wanted to get back with you right away. I got a message that you called!"

"Hi, I'm returning your phone call from (this morning) (yesterday afternoon). I'm glad to hear from you." ·

. . . .

31 Place a note on your phone as a reminder: "Stop. Think: Who am I calling and what is my purpose? Then dial!"

. . . .

32 If you notice any indications of the "treadmill syndrome"—an overly full schedule, stress, feeling overwhelmed, being caught in too many obligations, or having relationships and well-being that are suffering—stop yourself immediately and schedule a half-day for realignment. Review your personal and professional goals, values, accomplishments, and priorities. List all your current accountabilities and choose the items you need to revoke or renegotiate. Schedule your next seven days for handling priority items, recreational activities, relaxation time, and family and relationship time. Say no to any new requests for those seven days. At the end of that time you can consider requests again as long as you remember to first ask yourself the following questions:

1. How well will this fit into my schedule and plans?

2. How will this support my personal and professional goals?

3. Will this enhance or take away from my well-being, fulfillment, and sense of purpose?

. . . .

33 Choose a networking event to attend over the next two weeks, RSVP, schedule it in your time management planner, and prepare for the event by identifying the following:

❑ Your purpose for attending the event

❑ What you want to accomplish

❑ The introduction that will best serve your purpose and be suited to this group

❑ Suitable conversation generators you are comfortable using

❑ The knowledge that you have your pen and a sufficient supply of business cards handy

CHAPTER

16

ASK AND YE SHALL RECEIVE:
BE EFFECTIVE WITH YOUR REQUESTS

34 ASK FOR AND USE THE SUPPORT OF OTHERS.

> 66 *You were born into a sea of life existing in harmony with all others. You usually do things best when you do them with others, in cooperation, mutual trust, joy, and satisfaction.* 99
>
> Robert Conklin
> As quoted in Og Mandino,
> *Og Mandino's University of Success*

There are people all around you who can contribute to you in some way. Asking for and using the support of others is a significant step in eliminating the Lone Ranger mentality. When you are stuck, have a difficult personal or business problem, or want to enhance your skills in a particular area, ask for assistance from others. Another person can often provide objective support and valuable insights. Most people come up against the same problems or barriers to producing results. By calling for assistance you can often resolve these problems quickly and easily.

To ask for and accept support requires that you be open, vulnerable, coachable, and willing to learn. Realize that you do not have to have all the answers and are not expected to be an expert at everything. We live in a quickly changing world and what we learned as "tried-and-true" ways of operating may not be as effective or efficient today as they once were. Be open and willing to learn new ideas, new skills, and improved ways of operating to adjust to the changing trends of society and the business environment.

One type of support available is to have someone be your "coach." Coaching has been an effective means of accomplishing results in athletics. Athletes would not consider approaching a game or athletic feat without a coach to help guide, direct, give feedback, and support their success. You can use the same concept in various areas of your life. Would it serve to turn your health over to a fitness coach, nutrition coach, or doctor whom you trust? A financial coach can be the impetus for you to set up your budget, plan your retirement, and manage your finances so that you can attain financial independence. A business coach can be of great value to entrepreneurs and sole proprietors by providing objective feedback, support that keeps you on target, and insurance against falling back into the Lone Ranger mode. Consider using the services of a coach for any project or aspect of your life, as an effective way to manage yourself and set yourself up for success.

Stop thinking that if you want a job done right you have to do it yourself. Instead, see how you can best get the job done with the support and assistance of others. Do not automatically respond to offers of support with "Everything is handled," "That's okay, I can do it," or "I don't need anything." When people offer support, accept their help if it truly serves you. People love to contribute. Let them contribute to *you!*

35 MAKE REQUESTS OF YOUR NETWORK IN A CLEAR, CONCISE, AND NONDEMANDING MANNER.

66 *One person with a need contacts another with a resource and networking begins.* **99**

Jessica Lipnack and Jeffrey Stamps
The Networking Book

People will appreciate your ability to make clear, concise requests. A clear request makes it easier for them to respond with the best idea or contact for you.

Give people sufficient information to respond to your request without overloading them with data. Do not go overboard with too many stories, explanations, or extraneous facts. Once people respond to your request with interest and questions, you can give them additional information.

Generally, the more specific you can be, the easier it is for people to respond. If your request is too broad or general, people may feel confused or uncertain and think that they have no way to help. However, it may be that the request was not specific enough to "trigger" their thinking. Being specific generates a trigger or prompter that helps people to identify the contact or idea that will best support you.

A request that includes a hidden agenda, expectation, or manipulation is not a powerful, productive request. Even though people may respond to this type of request, they will not experience the trust and empowerment that is important in building strong networking relationships. Make requests, not demands, and people will be empowered and respond with true enthusiasm. Following are some examples:

Demanding	"I need you to give me . . ."
Empowering	"I am looking for . . . and thought you might . . ."
Vague	"I would like to contact good prospects for my business."
Clear	"My ideal client is . . . Who do you know who . . . ?"

Manipulative	"If you will . . . I will . . ."
Empowering	"I have some people to refer to you who . . . And keep me in mind when you meet people who . . ."
Hesitant	"I know you're busy and probably won't have time and I don't want to bother you, but . . ."
Straightforward	"I would like your assistance, if possible. Any amount of time you can give me will be appreciated."
Too broad	"I am looking for a job. Who can you recommend that I talk to?"
Specific	"I am looking for a job with a . . . company that can use my . . . expertise. Who do you know who . . . ?"
Confusing	"Do you think you could help me sell some of my widgets to people who have gadgets?"
Clear	"I want to contact people who are looking for widgets to better . . . Who do you know who I could call?"

If you make demands rather than requests, you set yourself up for disappointment. Realize that sometimes people can respond and sometimes they cannot or may not. Although it is important to know what you want, it is just as important to remember that your goals can be accomplished in various ways. When one door is closed, look for another avenue of opportunity. Your success will not depend on one person, one contact, or one response. There are always more opportunities available, although you may have to refocus and find a new direction to pursue.

Before you make a request, take a minute to ask yourself, "What is it that I really want?" Notice your gut-level response and design your request to ask for what you really want. A request that comes from the heart conveys a sincerity and enthusiasm that encourages people to respond.

36 CONSISTENTLY FIND OPPORTUNITIES TO ASK, "WHO DO YOU KNOW WHO . . . ?"

> **66** *Ask, and it shall be given you.* **99**
>
> **St. Matthew 7:7**

When asking for contacts, it is important to word your request to generate the best response. For example, "Who do you know who . . . ?" is a more effective question than "Do you know anyone who . . . ?" It is easy to respond to "Do you know anyone who . . . ?" with an automatic yes or no. The question "Who do you know who . . . ?" makes people begin to think about who they know, which creates a greater possibility for a response.

Powerful Networking Questions

"Who do you know who . . . ?"

"Who do you know who I should know (given the following circumstances) . . . ?"

"Who do you know who knows . . . ?"

"Who do you know who would benefit from . . . ?"

"Who would you recommend I contact about . . . ?"

"I would like to know who you would recommend for . . ."

"I am looking for . . . Who do you know who . . . ?"

"I would like to know the names of people you know who . . ."

When you make this type of request, be specific. Do not just say, "Who do you know who could use my product or service?" Be clear and explicit about what type of person you want to contact, for example:

"Who do you know who offices in an executive suite in the west area of town and is pleased with her arrangement?"

"Who do you know who is a partner with a local CPA firm whose accountants could generate more business by learning how to network effectively?"

"Who do you know in a professional association who we could contact about speaking at the association's regional or national convention?"

"Who do you know who I should know given that we are writing our first book, which is scheduled for completion this year?"

"Who do you know who has successfully submitted articles for publication in national magazines and periodicals?"

"Who do you know who is an independent representative for a network marketing company and who depends on effective networking to build his business?"

These types of questions can be asked in most networking situations. Be aware of the opportunity to make requests at the appropriate time in every call or contact by tuning into your intuition. By skillfully asking questions, you will consistently open the door to leads and opportunities.

When your requests are made graciously and appropriately, a feeling of respect, honor, and opportunity is conveyed. With the right wording and perceptive timing, you can ask people for support with ease and confidence. People really do like to be asked. Think about how you feel when someone in your network asks you for a contact or idea. Are you pleased to know that she thinks enough of you and her relationship with you to ask for your ideas or assistance? If you feel pleased, honored, and acknowledged when others approach you for assistance, let it be a reminder to you to ask. Asking is a way to empower, include, and recognize the people in your network for their resourcefulness.

37 FOLLOW UP PROMPTLY ON LEADS.

66 *Intentions count as nothing if we do not translate them into action.* **99**

Marsha Sinetar
Elegant Choices, Healing Choices

A major pitfall regarding networking is to get so involved with the process that you don't take time for the follow-up. Once you have been given a lead, gather the appropriate information, do your preparation, and promptly pursue the lead. It is easier to make the contact right away than it is to wait and then have to regenerate the energy and enthusiasm later. When follow-up activity begins to stack up, your chances of missing out on an opportunity increase.

A lead is just like a package you receive. You do not know whether the package contains gold, silver, or paper until you take the time to unwrap it and discover what is inside. A lead is similar in that you do not know what the opportunity will be until you take the time to pursue it and discover what is there.

Prompt follow-up will enhance your reputation as a reliable networker. People will remember you as someone who is organized, responsive, and action oriented. Develop prompt follow-up as a habit and it will become an easy and natural part of your networking effectiveness.

Some of the reasons people give for not promptly following up on leads include *forgetfulness, disorganization, being too busy,* and *fear of rejection.* If you forget, then as soon as you remember, follow up. If you have missed out on leads because of disorganization, get organized or hire someone to organize your office and procedures for you.

If you are a slave to a busy schedule, stop and reevaluate your projects and priorities and set up a time management system that works. If you are involved in a busy project but don't want to lose the lead, there are two good options: (1) make the initial contact, explain your situation, and schedule a future date for follow-up, or (2) make a reminder note, including all pertinent information, on a future date in your time management system.

If you fear rejection, think of networking as a game of discovery and each request as a stepping-stone. A "no" helps you know which direction to take next and gets you one step closer to "yes." Remember to let go of expectations and don't take a "no" answer personally. Then you will be able to follow up with enthusiasm rather than fear.

It is up to you to qualify the leads that are given to you. You do not need to accept leads hastily or automatically. Gather information from the person giving the lead to see if it is an appropriate contact for you. If it is not, express your thanks and explain why you will not be able to follow through on it at that time. When you do accept a lead, take the responsibility to follow up promptly and appropriately.

It is a compliment to the person who gives you a lead to be prompt and responsive. People want to have their leads used. The more prompt and responsive you are, the more likely it is that people will want to give you more leads.

38 GAIN VALUE FROM EVERY CONTACT.

> 66 *There is abundance of opportunity*
> *for the man who will go with the tide,*
> *instead of trying to swim against it.* 99
>
> **Wallace D. Wattles**
> *The Science of Being Great*

Every contact you make is an opportunity for gathering valuable information. Your ability to gather information will be enhanced when you plan ahead, are clear about your purpose, and stay tuned into possibilities during a conversation. The values that you gain from a contact can include:

An appointment

A sale

A new contact

Information that supports your project

Additional leads

Ideas that contribute to your work

Learning something that will help you to be more effective in future networking interactions

Your proficiency in asking questions and generating conversation will support your effectiveness in gaining value from every contact. Ask questions such as:

"Who do you know who . . . ?"

"What do you recommend?"

"How could what I have to offer support you?"

"Do you have a contact in . . . who I could call?"

Flexibility is important here; go with the flow and be willing to alter your agenda to gain value from the interaction. Do not allow yourself to go down a dead-end street when there are road signs and side streets that can lead you to new opportunities.

Every contact is a chance for you to grow, develop, learn, and prosper. Through your networking experience, you can become proficient in gaining value from every contact.

When You Don't Know What Is Next, Ask!–Sandy Vilas

In the mid eighties I had a real estate syndication firm in Houston; after a couple of tough years of long hours and hard work, I decided to close the firm. After making the final decision over a weekend, I went in on Monday morning, told the staff, and sat down at my desk with a major question on my mind: "Now what?" I had been so focused on my business that I had not even given any thought as to what I would do next.

My confidence, morale, and self-esteem were suffering from the blow of closing the company and I reached out to call Bill Hyland, an old friend who was the branch manager of an E. F. Hutton office in Naples, Florida. Bill and I had been in the brokerage business together in Cleveland, Ohio, and our relationship went back many years.

After telling Bill about my situation, I asked him for his opinion regarding what he thought would be a good career direction for me. He suggested that with my skills and experience, a job as an in-house wholesaler for a major brokerage firm would be ideal. This job would give me an opportunity to travel, give presentations, and sell, all of which he knew I enjoyed.

While we were talking, Bill got another phone call and he recommended that I get back with him to talk more about this career idea. I vowed to review my network, make a list of contacts who could support my job search, and call Bill later in the week.

Meanwhile, as president of my local college alumni association, I was responsible for calling twenty alumni that day regarding our annual dinner the following weekend. So I put my current woes aside to make my phone calls. The first name on my list was Mike Gibbons, who was the executive vice president of a regional brokerage firm headquartered in Houston. Mike indicated that he would not be able to attend the alumni dinner and we spent a few minutes covering other items of interest. Then, as we were about to close the conversation, I recalled my earlier conversation with Bill and said, "Oh, by the way, I am looking for a job as an in-house wholesaler for a major brokerage firm. Do you have any ideas for me?" The immediate response was a long, suspenseful pause, and then he recovered and told me that he had just lost his manager of financial services and he asked me to come in that afternoon for an interview.

A week later I had the job, and I worked there as manager of financial services for two years. The job was a great opportunity and learning experience for me. I had a very competent and professional staff and we had a lot of fun and success together.

This story is a great example of several of the principles of power networking: First, I gave up the Lone Ranger mentality and called for help. Often, when we are in distress, upset, or in major transition, it can be difficult to regain our own sense of clarity, wisdom, and direction. By calling a friend with whom I had worked years earlier and who knew me well, I was able to gain some objective, personal, and valuable support. Without this phone call, I would not have had the ability to make the request that led to my next job.

Second, on the day that I was "down and out" about closing my company, I continued to participate, contribute, and fulfill my commitment to my alumni association. I could easily have said to myself, "I don't want to do this," "I don't feel like it," or "I'll do this another time." Instead, thank goodness, I made the calls and the "boomerang effect" revealed itself once again. Just as a boomerang always comes back, in networking "what goes around comes around."

Third, I remembered to ask and my request was specific. Even though I felt unsure of myself and had very little knowledge of the job I was asking about, the thought came to mind and I asked. No story or explanation was needed and yet a golden opportunity appeared.

Does this sound like good luck!? Yes, when you consider that good luck is the result of participation, good timing, vulnerability, giving up the Lone Ranger mentality, and trusting the boomerang effect.

Statistically, over 70 percent of all jobs are found through networking and 100 percent of my jobs have been found through my network. Networking will not only enhance your personal and professional endeavors; it can also help you attain the perfect job for your career path.

PLAN YOUR ACTION; ACT ON YOUR PLAN

34 Developing a "networking action plan" will help you plan ahead so that you are considering all the tasks involved and all the resources that you can call on to assist you with your goal. Write a networking action plan for one of the goals that you identified in item 6. Take a blank sheet of paper and write your goal at the top of the page. Then make a list of all the tasks and action items that it will take to accomplish that goal. Once you have listed these tasks, to the right of each one write the names of the people you can contact for support, information, or assistance. Construct a networking action plan for each of your one-month goals. (Do the same thing for the other goals either now or at a later date.) Make a note in your time management system to contact at least one of the identified resources each day of the week.

. . . .

35 List five contacts you are going to call (as identified in item 34). Identify your purpose in calling them and write a clear, concise request that will prompt the response that you want.

Goal	Resource Person	Result Wanted	Request to Make
_____	_____	_____	_____
_____	_____	_____	_____
_____	_____	_____	_____
_____	_____	_____	_____
_____	_____	_____	_____

36   Make a list of clients and/or friends you can call to ask for referrals. Write and refine your "Who do you know . . . ?" request and make at least one call per day.

. . . .

37   When you are given a lead or referral, make a note in your time management system immediately regarding the follow-up action.

. . . .

38   Follow up with someone you have been hesitant to contact, and approach the call with an open mind regarding what he might do for you and what you can do for him.

IT'S NOT WHO YOU KNOW; IT'S WHO KNOWS YOU:
CREATE VISIBILITY THROUGH PARTICIPATION

39 BECOME A MEMBER OF A PROFESSIONAL ORGANIZATION.

66 *There is nothing like sharing a common purpose to build human relationships.* **99**

John F. Raynolds III and Eleanor Raynolds
Beyond Success

Join a professional organization and you will enhance your opportunity to expand your network as well as to develop your personal and professional skills. Clubs and organizations provide a place to meet like-minded people and develop yourself as a networker.

One type of professional organization that can be of value is the association for your particular industry. This organization can provide easy access to new trends, a strong network of career opportunities, and high-level contacts. It also allows you to have an impact not only on your business but on your industry. As your industry grows stronger, you and your business will benefit as well. Membership in an industry association is an expression of your commitment to your profession, and it will assist you in developing stronger relationships with your peers.

Since many associations have national and local chapters, membership greatly improves your network by providing immediate access to national and international contacts. National conferences can be a resource for dramatically expanding your business influence.

In addition to industry associations, professional networking organizations, chambers of commerce, and civic clubs are available in cities large and small all across the country. Choose wisely the group or club that best fits your purpose, values, and personal style. Through participation in professional organizations, millions of people across the country have received invaluable support, ideas, referrals, contacts, and friendships. When you discover the club or organization that is a fit for you, you may find yourself with an extended family that contributes to you in all areas of your life.

People who belong to professional organizations are generally the type of people who like to participate and contribute. Your participation in organizations will generate rich relationships, community service opportunities, and exceptional business growth.

40 SERVE ON A COMMITTEE OR BOARD OF AN ORGANIZATION.

> **66** *Membership in an organization is only as good as one's participation in the organization.* **99**
>
> **Ronald L. Krannich and Caryl Rae Krannich**
> *Network Your Way to Job and Career Success*

Serving on a committee or board of an organization provides an enhanced opportunity to learn, grow, participate, and contribute. As in other aspects of your life, the more you participate in organizations, the more you will receive. Participating fully will increase the rewards, satisfaction, and value that you experience from your membership.

As a committee or board member, you create more visibility for yourself while gaining new stature as a participant, contributor, and leader. You will be known as a giver, not just a taker. You will broaden your own horizons and expand your experience as a leader and networker. Participation through leadership provides a solid foundation for power networking.

41 REGULARLY GIVE REFERRALS TO AND MAKE REQUESTS OF YOUR NETWORK.

> 66 *The best part about networking is that everyone wins because everyone helps everyone else.* 99
>
> **Jan F. Triplett**
> *Networker's Guide to Success*

Being a power networker means being responsive to the people and circumstances around you. You can nurture and reinforce your network consistently with support. Look for opportunities, train yourself to pay attention, listen to what people are saying, and find out how to be of service. Most people are not comfortable asking for support, so you may need to find out for yourself how you can support them by asking questions. Take every opportunity to ask the following questions:

"What do you need?"

"How can I help?"

"What can I do for you?"

"How can I serve you?"

"What support would be most beneficial to you right now?"

The key to supporting others successfully is to listen with interest and take the initiative to offer referrals and support whenever you perceive a need. Be aware of the people and activities going on around you and use your intuition and perception to know when to offer your support to others. Whenever you meet someone, think about who would be the best person for her to talk to or meet. People will be truly honored and impressed by your responsiveness and willingness to give something to them. You will notice that a powerful momentum is generated by your willingness to give leads and referrals regularly.

Be sure that the support you offer is not just a way of "looking good" but is truly something that can be beneficial and valuable. Sometimes your support and ideas will be used successfully and sometimes they won't. Although networking offers no guarantees, you can be assured that by continuing to offer support to the people in your network, successes will happen and powerful networking relationships will develop.

42 BE AWARE OF AND USE THE "THREE-FOOT RULE."

❝ The way to build self-confidence is to start doing things you're not sure you can do. . . . Seize the day and get started and stay with it, and things will get easier from there.❞

Paul Williams
Da Energi

The "three-foot rule" states that anyone who is within three feet of you is a potential candidate for conversation and networking. Think about the three-foot radius around you and how many people come within that radius during your day. You may not normally think about networking with these people, and yet they can be approached in an easy, natural way. When you are in elevators, grocery store lines, reception areas, and restaurants, there are usually people within your three-foot radius. You can say hello or make a simple statement that leads to conversation. Don't force people to talk; simply be friendly and provide the opportunity for conversation.

As a society, we have isolated ourselves in many ways and often do not even know our neighbors. The cautionary words we heard as children, "Do not talk to strangers," can be adapted to include the discernment and wisdom we have as adults to react appropriately to our special circumstances and situations. Rather than isolating yourself, with the proper discernment you can take advantage of opportunities to approach people in suitable situations.

If you do not already talk to people within your three-foot radius, you may find it uncomfortable at first. However, once you begin to step out of your comfort zone, you may realize that pleasure, fun, and opportunities arise from saying hello and engaging in conversation with the people around you.

Be aware of the many people you come in contact with throughout your day. You can naturally and easily learn to reach out to these people in a comfortable and gracious way.

43 CONSISTENTLY REEVALUATE AND ADD TO YOUR NETWORK.

> 66 *Networking is not a one-time task,*
> *but a constant technique, an on-going*
> *process.* 99
>
> **Anne Boe and Bettie B. Youngs**
> *Is Your "Net" Working?*

A network is continually shifting, growing, and taking on new direction. It is not something that, once established, is set for life. You must treat your network as a live organism that functions only with your help. Keep the momentum going by reevaluating your network on a regular basis and adding to your network daily, weekly, or monthly as you meet people.

To reevaluate your network, sit down at least once a year (the first of the year is ideal) and review your list of contacts, update your name-and-address list, and clean out your business card file. Depending on your system, you may transfer people from one list to another, moving them from the full computer list to your current "hot" list or vice versa.

While you are reviewing your network, make changes on your network diagram and review your goals and projects for the upcoming year. Make sure that you include people on your handy "hot" list who are ideal contacts for your current year's focus. There will also be people with whom you have developed very strong and powerful relationships over the past year who will be obvious strong links in your network no matter what projects are current priorities in your life.

In the reevaluation process, identify who you want to have in your network and determine how to best make that connection. You want to include the people in your network who can best help you to meet your goals with ease and efficiency.

Whenever there is a change in your career, a new focus in your life, or a new project on the horizon, you should do a review and reevaluation of your network. Redesign your network to stay closely aligned with your goals and who you are as a networker.

NETWORKING —IN— ACTION

Living the "Three-Foot Rule"– John Demartini

The opportunity to meet new people and develop relationships exists in many places: in planes, restaurants, reception areas, and elevators, just to name a few. Power networkers use the three-foot rule to say hello to the people around them, thus initiating interesting conversations and generating new opportunities. Our friend John Demartini has used the three-foot rule in a very unique way.

John is a chiropractor, author, internationally known speaker, and workshop leader. He had moved his practice from West Houston to the Transco Tower in the Galleria and was looking for a creative way to generate a clientele at his new location. He came up with a unique idea—a workshop for the elevator! To get to John's office on the fifty-second floor, there is an express elevator to the fifty-first floor, and then a second elevator that goes to his office on the fifty-second floor. John timed the express elevator and designed a miniworkshop that lasted forty-eight seconds, the length of time that it took the elevator to go from the ground floor to the fifty-first.

When John arrived for work in the morning, he waited for a crowd to gather and made sure that he was the last person in the elevator. As he stepped on the elevator facing the group, they expected him to turn around and face the door, but he didn't. Instead he quickly started into his presentation and delivered his forty-eight-second workshop to his captive audience. After their initial surprise, they warmed up to John, enjoyed the presentation, and got their morning off to a great start. John's bold marketing strategy paid off in a big way. He developed new clients, speaking engagements, book and tape sales, and friends.

Even though John is a gregarious and dynamic person, this was a step out of his comfort zone. However, he was willing to take the risk, expand his horizons, and thus expand his base of contacts, clients, friends, and resources. Since then, John has developed and expanded his business to include a professional speaking and seminar schedule on an international scale.

We are not recommending elevator workshops, but we hope that this story will inspire and encourage you to step out of your comfort zone. Take the risk; try something new! We have made many valuable and enjoyable contacts on planes, in elevators, and at all types of events. Make yourself available to others by taking the first step in your three-foot radius. Initiating conversations with others in unlikely places is an enjoyable way to expand your network.

A "Net" You Can Bank on–Sandy Vilas

One of the most rewarding and enjoyable experiences of our lives has been our involvement and participation in The Dover Club and The Windsor Club. These are networking organizations whose purpose is to support the businesses, financial advancement, and success of their members. And they have gone beyond just business support; they are a team and a family.

One of the club members had a loan at a bank that was taken over by the Federal Deposit Insurance Corporation and he was concerned that they would call his note. Although he has a very successful business, he did not have the large volume of available cash that would be required to pay off the note.

After hearing about the situation, one club member called another who called another and an idea was conceived. The member with the loan was told that the club members had asked to be notified if the loan was called so that *all sixty members* of the club could meet with him at an appointed time at his bank to cosign the note!

Needless to say he was surprised and touched by the offer. And he was not the only one; the club members who offered the support were also moved by the realization of the level of commitment of the members to each other. His note was never called and thus we never had that meeting at his bank. Afterward, however, there was a new level of awareness, appreciation, and respect in our club because we all had had the opportunity to express our commitment to each other's success.

Networking clubs can have a dramatic impact on you, your business, and your city. If there is no club available in your city or area, start one. If you would like assistance, write us at the address on the order form in the back of this book. Joining and participating in a club of this type can dramatically affect all facets of your life!

PLAN YOUR ACTION:
ACT ON YOUR PLAN

39 Write your answers to the following questions: "What are my interests and goals in joining a professional organization?" and "Based on this, what type of professional organization would be the best fit for me?" Ask the people in your network and call your local Chamber of Commerce for phone numbers of the organizations that are prospects based on your answers to the questions.

. . . .

40 Once you have joined an organization, schedule a lunch meeting with one of the officers to learn about the club's activities and committees in order to decide where you can best participate.

. . . .

41 Place a note on your phone that says, "Ask, ask, ask! Who do you know who . . . ? How can I help you?"

. . . .

42 Say hello to one person per day who is in your three-foot radius and record what happens in the "notes" section of your daily planner.

. . . .

43 Decide to review your network on a quarterly, semiannual, or annual basis. Based on your decision, write "reevaluate network" in the appropriate places in your time management planner.

CHAPTER

18

LIFE IS EITHER A DARING ADVENTURE OR NOTHING:
DEVELOP A PERSONAL NETWORKING APPROACH

 44 TRUST AND FOLLOW YOUR INTUITION.

> ❝*Tune into your heart; you know all the answers.* ❞
>
> **Marsha Sinetar**
> *Elegant Choices, Healing Choices*

Your intuition can assist you in responding to opportunities with power and clarity. When you learn to trust that gut feeling or inner voice, you will be more flexible, perceptive, and adaptable to the situations around you.

Following your intuition is the best way to develop trust and awareness of your own natural instincts. Your instincts will tell you when things are not going well, when it is time to regroup, when to offer support, and when to take the initiative to ask for what you want. Strong intuition will keep you keenly aware of how to respond to the people and opportunities around you.

You have the ability to be perceptive and in tune with the people around you. Allow your "heart" to speak to you and show you the way.

45 BECOME COMMITTED TO THE SUCCESS OF THE PEOPLE IN YOUR NETWORK.

> **66** *Networking requires commitment and patience.* **99**
>
> **Anne Boe and Bettie B. Youngs**
> *Is Your "Net" Working?*

Commitment is a powerful generator of energy, momentum, action, and results. As Goethe said, "Until one is committed, there is hesitancy." However, once you have made a commitment, "providence moves" and things start to happen as you become more aware of opportunities to serve the people in your network.

Through your own commitment to the success of the people in your network, you will create a network of successful people. You will develop stronger links in your network when you support the success of others; as those around you become more successful, they will have more experience, support, and resources to give back to you. The people in your network will be even more valuable to you as their success grows.

The stronger your commitment, the greater will be the foundation on which your network grows and develops. Don't build your house on sand; build it on a strong commitment, creating a networking foundation that will serve you for the rest of your life. You will discover that when you give more than you expect to receive, you will get even more than you need. Being committed to the success of others will ensure your success.

Your commitment to the people in your network will come back to serve you tenfold. Author and lecturer Gerald Jampolsky says, "Giving is receiving." This is true in networking as well as in other aspects of your life. The more you give in networking, the more satisfaction and opportunities you will receive. You will grow tremendously as a networker if you constantly look for opportunities for the people in your network. You are the hub of your network and therefore can be a source of empowerment and success for the people around you.

Identifying people as part of your network is a responsibility. Do not build a network of mere acquaintances but one with solid relationships where there is a commitment to mutual satisfaction and success.

46 BECOME KNOWN FOR THE HIGH LEVEL OF SERVICE YOU PROVIDE.

> **❝ You don't have to be in a service business to deliver service. Whatever you do, you are in some way, shape, or form giving service. And that service touches the lives of people everywhere. ❞**
>
> Ron McCann and Joe Vitale
> *The Joy of Service*

Providing a high level of service is essential for the success of your business and for your effectiveness as a networker. People like to be taken care of and offered a quality product. In addition, they want to know that the people they refer to you will be served in the best possible way.

Word-of-mouth advertising will happen automatically when you have satisfied customers. When you please them, you are giving them good reason to tell others about your services. And the best networking someone can do for you is to provide a personal testimonial and recommendation. As Anthony Putman emphasizes in *Marketing Your Services* (1990, p. 173), "Networking through satisfied customers will give you the best return for your marketing efforts."

Focus on giving people *more* than their money's worth. Make sure that the value and benefits of your service can be clearly seen. Your own commitment and expression of quality will attract quality people, contacts, and services back to you.

An extra benefit of being a powerful networker is that people will give *you* good service. They will make sure that you are served well because they know that if you are pleased you will be a source of referrals for them.

When a person sends you business, he is entrusting to you someone he values in his network. Make sure that you take special care of the referrals that are sent to you. If you expect people to trust you and send business to you, you must let them know that they can count on you for quality products and excellent customer service.

Our business culture has experienced exceptional growth in the service sector, and top-notch corporations in all industries are proving that quality service is key to their growth and success.

47 BECOME AN ACTIVE AND PERCEPTIVE LISTENER.

66 *Hearing is one of the body's five senses. But listening is an art.* **99**

Frank Tyger
As Quoted in Bobbi Sims,
   Making a Difference in Your World

Communication is one of the vital skills of a power networker and developing this skill is a lifelong process. Many people think of communication as simply developing their speaking ability. However, communication is the transfer of information, which includes more than just speaking—it includes listening.

The more you listen the more you learn, and the more opportunities you will have for networking. You may have heard that communication consists of only 7 percent verbal information and 93 percent body language, tone of voice, speed of delivery, and facial expressions. Enhance your ability to accurately respond to what people are communicating by paying attention to their words, actions, expressions, and tone of voice. You will be amazed at how much you learn when you practice skillful listening.

Listening is commonly viewed as a passive role; however, active listening will ensure that you are hearing what the other person wants to communicate to you. Active listening is a means of reflecting back or paraphrasing what the person said, so that what you "heard" is either verified or corrected. By using active listening in an easy and natural way, you will have fewer misunderstandings and misconceptions. You can employ this technique to confirm the appropriate action to take regarding a referral. Active listening phrases include:

"What I think I hear you saying is . . ."

"If I am understanding you correctly, it seems that Mr. Smith would be a good person for me to contact right away regarding . . ."

"So you think I should call . . . regarding . . . ?"

Give this type of verbal feedback to confirm the message so that you and the other party are clearly speaking the same language. Do not assume that you know what she means; check it out.

In networking, it is especially important to listen well. Many people either talk or think about what they are going to say during most of their conversations. What have they learned? Or better yet, what could they have learned had their attention been on listening and finding out more about the other person? What is the normal ratio of listening and talking in your interactions? If you tend to talk more than you listen, switch your focus. Listen, gather information, ask questions, and then listen some more. Notice the difference when you increase your listening skills. Being an active and perceptive listener will ensure you of valuable information, empowered fellow networkers, and greater follow-up opportunities.

48 OPERATE WITH INTEGRITY AND PROFESSIONALISM IN ALL YOUR INTERACTIONS AND ENDEAVORS.

66 *Speak with good purpose only.* **99**
Rolling Thunder, Indian wise man

Dealing with people in an honest and professional way provides others with assurance that they can confidently refer to you and do business with you. It is of utmost importance to operate with the highest regard and respect for the people in your network. If you treat people with courtesy and respect, they are more likely to operate the same way in return. Your integrity and professionalism will generate strength and trust in your relationships and business interactions. Speak with integrity regarding the quality of your product and the service that you offer. Do not overstate the benefits of your products or services. Sell to satisfy a need rather than because you need a sale.

Speak well of people or do not say anything. In other words, do not gossip. The test for gossip is whether you would still say something if the person you were talking about were standing next to you. And do not make negative statements regarding your competition. Speak about the benefits and value of your product or service and let others speak for themselves.

Be accountable for your actions by admitting errors, correcting mistakes or misunderstandings, and apologizing when appropriate. People appreciate networking with someone they can trust, who is as fair as possible, and who is willing to work things out when events do not go as planned.

Do not misuse networking. Be professional and trustworthy so that networking will be appreciated for the valuable tool that it is. Operate with people in such a way that they will experience the positive aspects of networking and convey them to others.

Give people the assurance that they can confidently refer to you or call on you. By operating with integrity and professionalism, you will be conveying a message of trust, partnership, and accountability that others will respond to.

49 APPROACH EACH CONTACT AND OPPORTUNITY WITH AN OPEN MIND.

> **❝** *Be so impressed with the value of a man that you treat even a beggar or a tramp with the most distinguished consideration.* **❞**
>
> **Wallace D. Wattles**
> *The Science of Being Great*

You cannot know with certainty what the end result will be when you make a contact or approach a new situation. Your willingness to approach people with an open mind will increase your chances of generating new opportunities through networking.

Notice when you have the following thoughts:

"He can't help me."

"She won't have any contacts regarding . . ."

"He doesn't look like someone who . . ."

"They obviously don't . . ."

"They probably wouldn't want to . . ."

Thoughts such as these can occur in situations where you do not really know a person, as well as in situations where you think you do know the person. In either case, these thoughts may cause you to miss a potential opportunity. Let go of preconceived notions and approach people with an open mind. Explore situations sufficiently to discover if there are possibilities. Facts, information, intuition, and experiences can help give you direction when situations are perceived with an open mind.

Networking is fun and exciting when you are willing to approach it with enthusiasm. It is like a treasure hunt in which you never know what you may find but in which you always enjoy the process. Discovering new links, opportunities, and resources can be a continual surprise and delight with a power networking lifestyle.

NETWORKING
—IN—
ACTION

There's More to People Than Meets the Eye

This poignant story, about a missed opportunity resulting from a judgment and a comparison, can be a reminder to keep an open mind regarding people and opportunities.

An elderly couple arrived at Harvard University requesting the opportunity to speak to the president of the college. The woman was dressed in a simple gingham dress and her husband was attired in a threadbare homespun suit. The secretary said that the president was not available. They replied that their business was important so she reluctantly said that they could wait.

The secretary had sized them up as country hicks and kept them waiting nearly half the day with very little courtesy, warmth, or interest. Finally, out of desperation, she allowed the couple in to see the president.

They explained to the president that their son had died accidentally after one year at Harvard. His schooling had meant so much to him that they wanted to erect a memorial to him on the campus. The president tersely replied that if they allowed a memorial for every student who had passed away, the campus would look like a cemetery. They explained that they did not just want a monument; they wanted to build a building in his name. The president informed them that there were $7.5 million dollars' worth of buildings on the campus, thinking that this would discourage them and speed them on their way.

At this point, the wife quietly said to her husband that perhaps they should do something else in memory of their beloved son. Mr. and Mrs. Leland Stanford left the president's office that day making plans to build their own university, which today is one of the finest institutions of higher learning in the country.

There is no way to know how many opportunities have been lost or ignored because of preconceived ideas or judgments. Give up judging situations and allow the value of each opportunity to reveal itself.

The Boomerang Effect in Networking–
Ann Knauth

The misunderstanding many people have about networking is that it is risky and may not pay off. We say that the boomerang effect is the guarantee of networking. The way the boomerang works is that when you give, participate, contribute, and support the people in your network, the benefits *will* come back to you. As with the boomerang, benefits may not come back in a straight line directly from the organization or individuals you gave to; however, they will come back to you. You have to trust and initiate the action by throwing the boomerang!

Ann Knauth heard our presentation on "The Ten Commandments of Networking" and was particularly intrigued by the idea of the boomerang effect. Very soon thereafter, a member of her professional women's organization gave her an opportunity to try it out.

Ann belongs to an organization of women in business who network and use each others' services. The interior designer in the club had a new job updating the look of a restaurant and asked Ann (who runs an architectural design firm) to visit the restaurant with her and review a sketch of the proposal she was going to present to the owner of the restaurant. She was especially interested in Ann's feedback regarding the carpentry work and color recommendations she was proposing.

Ann realized that it would take a few hours to drive to and from the location, join her fellow club member for lunch, and review the information. In the past Ann had felt that she needed to be rather protective of her billable time and careful not to give away her services. This time, she approached her lunch meeting with a new attitude and gave her feedback with no expectations, being content with the satisfaction of having responded to a fellow club member. Thinking about the concept of giving freely to support the people in her network, she decided to just do it and not expect anything in return!

Approximately eight weeks later, a friend of the owner of the restaurant walked into the restaurant and commented to the interior designer that he wanted some remodeling work done on his house. The interior designer recommended Ann and even scheduled a meeting where she introduced the prospective client to Ann.

Ann got that job and was called by this same interior designer within a few weeks for another lucrative project! Two weeks later she acquired another job through this same contact. Ann is now a true believer in the boomerang effect and she is also eagerly watching for opportunities on her remodeling jobs to recommend her fellow club member for interior design work.

And all this started as a simple request, a gracious response, a favor given with nothing expected. The ripple effect of networking can go on and on for you and the people in your network!

PLAN YOUR ACTION;
ACT ON YOUR PLAN

44 Practice following your intuition in small ways throughout your day. Notice and respond to your gut feelings, inclinations, and "sense" of things.

. . . .

45 Call someone you have not talked to in three months. Find out how she is doing and what you can do for her.

. . . .

46 List ten ways by which you can increase the quality of the product or service that you offer.

. . . .

47 In every conversation this week, pay extra attention to what people are saying through their words, body language, and tone of voice. Respond to what they are saying rather than what you are thinking.

. . . .

48 If someone asks you, "How is 'so-and-so'?" encourage him to call that person. Rather than talking about people, be a catalyst for people to network and stay in communication with one another.

. . . .

49 Think of someone you have been hesitant to contact and review in writing your purpose for the call with a sample script showing how you would like the conversation to go. Think about several possible results that would create value for you. Imagine that the call goes so well that its results are greater than your most optimistic thoughts. Remind yourself that anything is possible and make your phone call.

19

A WAY OF LIFE THAT WILL CHANGE THE WORLD: NETWORK TO ENHANCE YOUR WORLD

50 BECOME KNOWN AS A POWERFUL NETWORKER WITH AN ESTABLISHED AND RESOURCEFUL NETWORK.

> **66***A person who enables others to succeed is invariably sought after and respected.***99**
>
> **Arleen LaBella and Dolores Leach**
> *Personal Power*

As your network and your networking activities expand, you will become known as a powerful networker. When you are known for something, people will think of you and call on you. And when they know you have a strong network, they will be drawn to call on you because of the power that you exhibit through your resources. Your name will be linked with others who are resourceful networkers, once again creating a strong and expanding pool of resources.

When you are known as a powerful networker, people will call you with both requests and opportunities. Some requests will give you a chance to easily offer support to someone else. The opportunities may provide contacts, information, or ideas that are valuable to you.

Powerful networkers become known not only for their resourcefulness but for the qualities they portray that exemplify effective networkers. Those who network effectively today are resourceful people who produce results, contribute to others, and enjoy participating. Networkers are also known for being good with people, since that is what networking is all about—working with and supporting people. Others will relate to you as a caring and supportive person when you network effectively to serve the people around you.

By being "known," you will create greater opportunities for yourself and also will be the recipient of more opportunities that you can pass along to your network. This has an upward spiral effect: known, more leads, better known, more opportunities, better known, larger network, and so on.

51 USE NETWORKING TO BENEFIT YOURSELF AND OTHERS PERSONALLY AS WELL AS PROFESSIONALLY.

66 Networking will provide a strong bridge between personal and professional lives. 99

Anne Boe and Bettie B. Youngs
Is Your "Net" Working?

Many people think that networking is strictly for achieving professional goals and miss out on the benefits of networking in their personal endeavors. Networking can support all areas of your life and can contribute to making everything you do easier and more fun.

For example, if you want to locate a good place to vacation, let people in your network know what type of trip you are planning. You will get a first-hand account of a myriad of ideas on places to go, things to see, and people to contact. This holds true for almost anything you are looking for: a car, movies, good buys on products or services, and so on.

Networking is a valuable means of support for all areas of life: hobbies, recreation, finance, health, or personal development. Apply the same principles that work in your business networking to ensure that your personal goals will be fulfilled.

52 KEEP YOUR NETWORK IN THE FOREFRONT OF YOUR THINKING.

❝Get into the networking habit. Connecting yourself to one other person who will spread the word to another is a monumentally effective way to make a difference in the world. ❞

Wayne W. Dyer
You'll See It When You Believe It

To propel yourself from effective networking to consistently powerful networking, always keep your network in the forefront of your thinking. This approach will guarantee that new ideas and opportunities will be generated as you go through your day. With this awareness, you will discover endless opportunities for yourself and your network.

The words "I am looking for . . . ," "I need . . . ," or "I am dissatisfied with . . ." will trigger you to think about your network and take action. When you think of a response, take out your card and write on the back the name and number of a contact person. When you give referrals, remind people to use your name as a reference and give them as much helpful information about the referral as you can. Often it may be appropriate to call the person in your network first to let him know to expect a call.

Working with your network and learning how to support people will reinforce your ability to consistently keep your network in the forefront of your thinking. If you raise your level of networking consciousness, you will support your network to new levels of success. When your network is in the forefront of your thinking, you will have the benefit of having it with you wherever you go.

53 BECOME A ROLE MODEL FOR POWER NETWORKING.

> 66*Networkers never try to accumulate power; they circulate all that they have, and encourage others to do the same.*99
>
> **Wayne W. Dyer**
> *You'll See It When You Believe It*

Living your life as a role model for others can be a gratifying aspiration. Make a strong commitment to learn how to network powerfully and you will be on your way. As others notice your success, they will look to see what they can learn from what you are doing. As they adapt what they see to their situation and generate success, others will notice them. Being a role model creates a ripple effect that also generates larger and expanding circles of influence. Without generating any more energy than you normally would, you are contributing to an ever-expanding group of resources.

You are always teaching by example! You can be an example of effective networking skills and therefore teach a positive approach to networking. You never know who is watching or what they may notice.

54 SEE THE WORLD AS ONE BIG NETWORK.

❝Today we live in a world of over-lapping networks, not just a constel-lation of networks but a galaxy of networking constellations.❞

John Naisbitt
Megatrends

According to statistics, you are only four to five contacts away from anyone. Most people do not operate as though this is true, thus limiting their effectiveness and their possibilities. By using the people you know as connecting links to the people they know, you are creating a network of unlimited resources.

Imagine the intricate connections and interconnections among these networks all around the world. Every individual is linked in some way to the people around her, providing the basis for networks that tie our world together. This image of a worldwide network of people represents the richness of our resources and the power of our strength as individuals. It is through individuals connecting with one another throughout the world that a strong web of relationships exists in a global network.

If you want to achieve your goals in life, networking is the best way to accomplish results and have fun doing it. Making links from people you know to people they know keeps the world at your fingertips. This way of operating eliminates tunnel vision, the concept of cold calling, and the idea that you do not know anyone to contact. However, it is still up to you to reach out, take the first step, and use your relationships and contacts in a major way. Allow yourself to enjoy the magnitude of an arena that brings with it limitless opportunities.

The concept of global stepping-stones represents the idea that anyone you want to contact can be reached through the wise and effective use of your network in sync with this worldwide web of networks. Let this concept be your reminder to live your life as one who is connected to everyone in the world and you will discover a renewed vigor and excitement regarding networking.

55 MAKE NETWORKING A WAY OF LIFE.

❝ *You were born into a sea of life existing in harmony with all others. You usually do things best when you do them with others, in cooperation, mutual trust, joy, and satisfaction.* **❞**

Robert Conklin
As quoted in Og Mandino,
Og Mandino's University of Success

Networking is not just a way of interacting or a way of relating; it is a way of life that is designed around a strong foundation of relationships and supported by clarity of purpose and an attitude of service and contribution.

People have the opportunity every day to make choices about life. Developing a lifestyle with networking as the base indicates that you have already chosen a life of participation, contribution, and relationship. With this as the basis for your actions and interactions, you can easily respond to the choices that come your way to further the goals you have chosen for your life.

The truth is that people want to participate and contribute, to serve and support one another. They want a community, country, and world where people are working together rather than fighting, praising one another and celebrating accomplishments rather than hurting each other—where the quality of life is positive and rewarding rather than depressing and dangerous. How can we have this? How can we as individuals contribute to something that seems so big and appears to be beyond our grasp? We can start by networking with each other for the good of all. And we can develop our ability to communicate effectively, listen with interest, ask for support, and develop strong bonds within our families, communities, organizations, and society.

Take the plunge and make a commitment to network as a way of life. It is a golden opportunity that offers a "win-win" situation for everyone. Develop networking as your way of life and you will not only affect the people around you; you will also implement a ripple effect that will travel through the links in your network to other networks around the globe. Networking is more than just a good idea or an effective way to expand your business; it is an opportunity to create a lifestyle that will have an impact on you, the people around you, and the world we live in. Choose today to network as a way of life and enjoy the satisfaction of knowing that you have chosen wisely for yourself and your world.

NETWORKING —IN— ACTION

Networking: A Game of Discovery– Sandy Vilas

Networking is an exciting adventure. It is like a game of discovery; each time you are given an opportunity to make a move, you may discover hidden treasures. Even when the results you want to produce don't happen, the adventure can be rewarding and exciting. And you never know how the intricate maze of connections and interactions may one day loop around to support you on your particular path.

This story about how we connected with Harvey Mackay, best-selling author of *Swim with the Sharks Without Being Eaten Alive*, illustrates that maze and the excitement that comes from discovering new connections and making new friends.

Joe Vitale, a Houston author and book consultant, has been a major source of encouragement and support for us with our book. He is also great about sending us notes, clippings, and information about books, magazines, and articles on networking. One day, Donna got a note in the mail from Joe that said, "Harvey Mackay has a brand-new book out on networking entitled *The Harvey Mackay Rolodex Network Builder*. I thought you would be interested!" Donna went out that day and bought it, read it, and then passed it on to me.

I read the book right away and one of Harvey's stories particularly got my attention. In his book, Harvey tells how he used his vast network to help make the contacts that would bring together a group to purchase the Minnesota North Stars hockey team and thus keep the team in his hometown of Minneapolis. The reason the story jumped out at me was that I was pretty sure that one of the people Harvey referred to as part of the buying group was someone I had gone to prep school with thirty years earlier. I had only talked to Howard Baldwin twice since our prep school days. Both times I had read in the paper that he had either bought or sold a hockey team and I called to congratulate him.

After I read Harvey's book, I called Howard to see if he was the person Harvey was referring to, and sure enough, he was. I told Howard about the networking book we were writing and asked if he would be willing to help set up a phone conversation for me with Harvey. About a week later, I got a call back from Howard saying that Harvey was on a book tour, but he had my number and had agreed to call us sometime within the next few weeks.

We immediately put on our thinking caps regarding how to be prepared for that call. Donna and I reviewed our ideas about how Harvey could be a valuable resource for us. He might:

> Review our book and make recommendations regarding agents, publishers, book promotion, and so on
>
> Agree to provide a quote for the book or write the foreword
>
> Connect us with others in the writing and speaking industry
>
> Be available as a professional contact or mentor

We also reviewed the ways in which we could be a resource for Harvey. We might:

> Hand out announcements about his upcoming Houston seminar at meetings
>
> Provide him with organizational contacts for promotional speaking engagements
>
> Provide mailing labels for the people who had attended our workshops so that they could be sent a brochure about his seminar

It is clear from reading Harvey's books that he is an avid and powerful networker, so we knew that we had the common ground of a similar philosophy and belief in networking.

Just as Howard said, within a few weeks Harvey Mackay called! During thirty minutes of talking and getting to know each other, I asked him to review our book manuscript and he agreed. Then I offered my support by asking, "What can I do for you?" He responded that there was nothing he could think of, but as I said, Donna and I had done our homework. So I presented the idea to Harvey that we could help to promote his Houston seminar by providing his promotions team with the mailing labels of the Houston people who had attended our workshops. Harvey accepted our support and told us how to reach his promotions manager, who was in Houston arranging for and promoting the event. Four days later, Donna and I had lunch with Harvey's promotion manager, gave him the mailing labels, and made arrangements for him to visit our breakfast club.

We had a great time working with Harvey's promotion manager to get the word out about the Harvey Mackay seminar. And the boomerang came back to us through the people we met and the opportunity to briefly visit with Harvey prior to his Houston presentation. I have had several conversations with Harvey since, and he has generously given us recommendations and support regarding the book that you now have in your hand. Harvey responded as a valuable resource in three out of the four areas where we wanted support. More importantly, we added several wonderful new links to our network and gained a valuable contact and friend.

Networking may not always bring you the exact results you want precisely when you want them. However, there is always value gained when support is shared and new connections are established. Networking is a nurturing, building process. The seeds you are planting are quietly gaining strength. Just keep planting those seeds and be willing to stay around to enjoy the blossoms.

How It Began—And How It Has Grown– Donna Fisher

When I worked as executive director of the Houston Center for Attitudinal Healing, we sponsored a monthly luncheon in which people from the business community could learn about the work and purpose of the center. A volunteer and my personal friend, Joan Bolmer, brought a friend, Sandy Vilas, to one of these luncheons. Afterward, as other guests were leaving, I had an opportunity to talk with Sandy. He gave me five contacts—three regarding professional organizations to which I could give presentations, one within the medical community, and one regarding carpet that we needed for the center's children's annex. I was impressed. As I mentioned, we conducted these luncheons every month, with an average attendance of eight to twelve people. I always let people know how they could support the center, and yet typically the majority of the people came and left with thanks, appreciation, and encouragement for what we were doing. However, this person did much more than that. He listened, showed an interest, and responded immediately with names and phone numbers.

I sensed that these were "hot" leads I should follow up on right away. I did and I was right! The people he referred me to were helpful and responsive, and I scheduled speaking engagements right away at the three organizations he recommended. After getting back with Sandy to thank him for the referrals, I saw him at the presentations I gave and each time he gave me more ideas.

One of the speaking engagements I scheduled was with The Dover Club, which Sandy had founded four months earlier. I was so impressed with this group's enthusiasm and camaraderie that I soon applied for membership.

After several years, I left The Dover Club and became an adviser and member of a similar organization called The Windsor Club. I value my participation in The Dover Club and The Windsor Club and consider the support of these groups instrumental in the development and growth of Discovery Seminars and the "Power Networking" workshop.

Sandy and I have learned a lot from each other and through our participation in these networking organizations. Our qualities, talents, and strengths blend together to give us additional power and strength. We have learned the value of relationships, teamwork, and having clear dreams and goals. We have learned and experienced the value, power, and joy of networking in all areas of life. Networking is the way of life we choose and it is difficult now to imagine life any other way. Networking adds richness to our life, our relationships, and the work that we do. We are pleased and honored to be able to share our experience with you. Thank you and blessings to you in all your endeavors.

PLAN YOUR ACTION;
ACT ON YOUR PLAN

50 Call three people in your network and let them know that you are glad they are in your network. Ask the questions, "What do you need?" and "How can I help?"

. . . .

51 Think of your personal goals and identify several ways to include the people in your network in the accomplishment of your personal dreams.

. . . .

52 Imagine your mind as a computer with unlimited storage, immediate recall and retrieval, and an electronic antenna that triggers a data search in response to the words "I want . . . ," "I am looking for . . . ," or "I need . . ."

. . . .

53 Offer to be a mentor to someone.

. . . .

54 Think of someone you have not contacted because you thought he was out of your reach. Write down why you want to contact him, what you think he can do for you, and what you can possibly do for him. Identify ten people in your network to contact regarding links or ideas they might have for making this contact. Continue your research of your network until you have used your own global stepping-stones to make your connection!

. . . .

55 Keep a networking journal. Complete the "Plan Your Action; Act on Your Plan" items listed at the end of each chapter. Include stories, examples, quotes, affirmations, visualizations, and miracles in your journal.

PART

A LIFESTYLE FOR SUCCESS

66That man is a success who has lived well, laughed often and loved much; who has gained the respect of intelligent men and the love of children; who has filled his niche and accomplished his task; who leaves the world better than he found it whether by a perfect poem or a rescued soul; who never lacked appreciation of earth's beauty or failed to express it; who looked for the best in others and gave the best he had.99

Robert Louis Stevenson

CHAPTER

20

Planting the Seed

Consistent and persistent utilization of your networking approach will reap amazing benefits. If you join a networking club, don't look for a return right away. Focus on getting to know people, participating fully, and supporting others as best you can. Just as the major results of an exercise program happen after a certain period of time, the impact of your networking efforts will materialize and escalate with the consistent practice of these networking principles. Exercising becomes easier after awhile, and then you get to add time, weight, or distance to your exercise program. Similarly, your networking will also become easier, more natural, and more comfortable, allowing you to add more fun, excitement, and success to the rest of your life.

Networking is a lifestyle for success that will provide you with support for life. If, like so many others, you have not been using your resources and contacts fully to accomplish your dreams, then it is time to broaden your vision and activate your network. We encourage you to use the ideas in this book to develop your network as a dynamic source of energy and results.

We believe that networking will be around forever because people have a natural desire to serve and support one another. Networking consists of making links from person to person, giving with no expectations, sharing resources with others, and distributing information. It allows you to accept the opportunities that arise while you are simply doing what you do.

Please make sure that you work with the principles and ideas in this book long enough for them to bear fruit. Networking is like planting a seed, nurturing it, and patiently, eagerly, watching for it to grow. It is not something you "do" for one day, finding on the next day that the seed is a tree. It is a nurturing, time-building process, generating roots that continue to go deeper into the ground and branches that continue to reach higher up into the sky. As those roots and branches grow, you will experience more strength and power from your network and results will happen more easily and rapidly. Over time, asking, offering, giving, and receiving will become natural and easy for you; then you will know that you have developed a networking lifestyle that will enhance your life forever.

> 66 *You really have to live [networking], not just passing information on without it touching you or being touched by you. You are part of the totality, you are a seeker of truth, of what is good for the human race, of what will be our fate, of what will improve our fate. . . . It has to be deeply lived. Then you are a good networker.* 99
>
> **Robert Muller**
> **As quoted in Jessica Lipnack and Jeffrey Stamps,**
> *The Networking Book*

BIBLIOGRAPHY

Autry, James A. *Love and Profit*. New York: William Morrow, 1991.

Blanchard, Kenneth, and Norman Vincent Peale. *The Power of Ethical Management*. New York: William Morrow, 1988.

Boe, Anne, and Bettie B. Youngs. *Is Your "Net" Working?* New York: John Wiley, 1989.

Cohen, Alan. *The Dragon Doesn't Live Here Anymore*. South Kortright, N.Y.: Eden, 1981.

Cohen, Alan. *The Healing of the Planet Earth*. Awakening Heart Productions, 1987.

Cohen, Sherry Suib. *Tender Power*. Reading, Mass.: Addison-Wesley, 1989.

Dunn, David. *Try Giving Yourself Away*. Englewood Cliffs, N.J.: Prentice-Hall, 1970.

Dyer, Wayne W. *You'll See It When You Believe It*. New York: William Morrow, 1989.

Ferguson, Marilyn. *The Aquarian Conspiracy*. Los Angeles: J. P. Tarcher, 1981.

Heider, John. *The Tao of Leadership*. Atlanta: Humanics Limited, 1985.

Krannich, Ronald L., and Caryl Rae Krannich. *Network Your Way to Job and Career Success*. Manassas, Va.: Impact Publications, 1989.

LaBella, Arleen, and Dolores Leach. *Personal Power*. Boulder, Colo.: CareerTrack Publications, 1985.

Lao Tzu. *The Tao: The Book of Meaning and Life*. London: ARKANA, 1985.

Lipnack, Jessica, and Jeffrey Stamps. *The Networking Book*. New York: Routledge & Kegan Paul, 1986.

McCann, Ron, and Joe Vitale. *The Joy of Service*. Stafford, Tex.: Service Information Source Publications, 1989.

Mackay, Harvey B. *Swim with the Sharks Without Being Eaten Alive*. New York: Ivy Books, 1988.

Mackenzie, Alec R. *The Time Trap: Managing Your Way Out*. New York: AMACOM, 1990.

Mandino, Og. *Og Mandino's University of Success*. New York: Bantam Books, 1982.

Megill, Robert E. *May I Touch Your Life?* Tulsa, Okla.: Petroleum Publishing Company, 1979.

Morrison, Emily K. *Skills for Leadership: Working with Volunteers.* Tucson, Ariz.: Jordan Press, 1983.

Naisbitt, John. *Megatrends.* New York: Warner Books, 1982.

Peterson, Wilferd A. *The Art of Living Treasure Chest.* New York: Simon & Schuster, 1977.

Putman, Anthony O. *Marketing Your Services.* New York: John Wiley, 1990.

Raynolds III, John F., and Eleanor Raynolds. *Beyond Success.* New York: Master-Media Limited, 1988.

RoAne, Susan. *How to Work a Room.* New York: Shapolcky Publishers, 1988.

Robbins, Anthony. *Unlimited Power.* New York: Simon & Schuster, 1986.

Schwartz, David J. *The Magic of Thinking Big.* New York: Cornerstone Library, 1986.

Sher, Barbara, and Anne Gottlieb. *Teamworks!* New York: Warner Books, 1989.

Sims, Bobbi. *Making a Difference in Your World.* Gretna, La.: Pelican, 1984.

Sinetar, Marsha. *Elegant Choices, Healing Choices.* New York: Paulist Press, 1988.

Triplett, Jan F. *Networker's Guide to Success.* Austin, Tex.: Diener, Triplett and Associates, 1986.

Wattles, Wallace D. *The Science of Being Great.* Lakemont, Ga.: TriState Press Corps, 1982.

Wilson, Marlene. *Survival Skills for Managers.* Boulder, Colo.: Volunteer Management Associates, 1981.

INDEX

Acknowledgments: action plans and action steps for, 111–112; through calls, notes, and gifts, 104–105; case studies of, 108–110; daily receiving and giving of, 101–102; of inspiring people, 103; personalized notecards for, 106; receiving and acceptance of, 101–102, 107
Action list, daily, 117–119
Action plans and action steps, 70–72, 90–92, 98–99, 111–112, 127–129, 143–144, 154, 165, 179
Active listening, 158–159
Affection, 47
Agenda, written, 74
Aggression, fear of, 32–33
Appearance, personal, 73–74
Asking for support, 31
Assessment, on power networking, 51–55
Association, in memory recall, 82
Associations, professional: committee or board responsibilities in, 147; membership in, 145–146

Baldwin, H., 175–176
Blanchard, K., 118
Board membership, 147
Boe, A., 37, 47, 124, 156, 169
Bolmer, J., 177
Boomerang effect, 28, 124, 142, 163–164
Bush, B., 108–109
Business cards: action plans and action steps for, 98–99; appropriate exchange of, 95; case study of, 97; design of, 93–94; as follow-up reminders, 96; notations on, as memory joggers, 96; organization and retrieval of, 113–115; sufficient number of, 94

Calls. See Telephone calls
Case studies, 67–69, 87–89, 97, 108–110, 124–126, 141–142, 151–153, 162–164, 175–177
Coaching, 132
Cohen, A., 101
Cohen, S. S., 107
Commitment, to success of people in network, 156
Committee membership, 147

Communication: in conversation generators, 79–80; in giving and receiving acknowledgments, 101–107; in introductions, 81–83; and listening, 158–59; in referrals and making requests of network, 148; of requests for network, 131–144, 148; and role of host, 84–85; in self-introduction, 75–78, 87–89; by telephone, 104–105, 119–121
Computer technology, 46–47, 114
Confucius, 20
Conklin, R., 131, 173
Contacts, asking for, 135–136
Conversation generators, 79–80
Courtesy. See Graciousness and courtesy
Cross (A. T.) Company, 106

Daily action list, completion of, 117–119
Database management system, 114
Demartini, J., 58, 151–152
Denver, J., 64
Devodier, J., 67–68
Diagram of network, 66
Dover Club, The, 9–10, 18, 152–153, 178
Dress, 73–74
Dunn, D., 103, 104
Dyer, W. W., 15, 40, 170, 171

Ease in groups, 79–80
Efficiency: of networking, 47; and time management system, 116
Emerson, R. W., 62, 86
Expertise, personal, 62

Fears: of appearing pushy and aggressive, 32–33; of being cold and impersonal, 33; of looking weak or needy, 31; of obligation, 30; of rejection, 29–30, 137–138; of time needed for networking, 32
Feedback. See Acknowledgments
Feray, M., 87–89
Ferguson, M., 44
Focus, in memory recall, 82
Follow-up: and business cards, 96; on leads, 137

Gifts, nurturing through, 104–105
Global nature of power networking, 45–48, 172

Goals, personal, 65, 169

Graciousness and courtesy: action plans and action steps for, 90–92; case study of, 87–89; and conversation generators, 79–80; and ease in groups, 79–80; and examples of courtesy and good manners, 86; and focus on people as they are introduced, 82–83; and memory recall, 82–83; and personal appearance and presentation, 73–74; and promotion and creation of visibility of self and business, 85; in receiving and accepting acknowledgments, 107; and reintroductions, 81; and role of host, 84–85; and self-introduction, 75–78

Grass-roots organizations, 46

Groups: conversation generators in, 79–80; ease in, 79–80

Hayes, R., 40
Heider, J., 50
Hoppe, J., 41
Host, role of, 84–85
Hyland B., 141–142

Impersonality, fear of, 33
Independence. *See* Lone Ranger mentality
Index card system, for organizing and retrieving network, 114
Inspiration, acknowledgment of, 103
Integrity, in all interactions and endeavors, 160
Interdependence, thoughts concerning, 24–25
Introductions: and focus on people as they are introduced, 82–83; and reintroductions, 81; and remembering names, 82–83; and self-introduction, 75–78, 87–89
Intuition, 155

Jampolsky, G., 156

Khalsa, H. S., 41
KISS rule (Keep It Short and Simple), 76
Knauth, A., 163–164
Korda, M., 73
Krannich, C. R., 40, 147
Krannich, R. L., 40, 147

La Bella, A., 167
Lao Tzu, 61
Leach, D., 167
Leads, follow-up on, 137–138

Lipnack, J., 40, 133
Listening: and active listening, 158–159; and focus on people as they are introduced, 82–83
Lone Ranger mentality: change from, to power networker, 63–64; definition of, 23; ideas counteracting, 24–25; ideas supporting, 23–24; and requests for support, 131–132, 142

McCann, R., 63, 157
Mackay, H., 96, 115, 175–177
Mackenzie, A. R., 116
Malloch, D., 113
Management. *See* Self-management
Manners, examples of, 86. *See also* Graciousness and courtesy
Matthew, St., 135
Megill, R. E., 119
Memory recall: of names, 82–83; and notations on business cards, 96
Mongrels, networking. *See* Networking mongrels
Morrison, E. K., 65
Muller, R., 14, 184
Murray, E., 109–110

Naisbitt, J., 41, 43, 47, 66, 172
Neediness, fear of, 31
Network diagram, 66
Networking: abuse or misuse of, 21–22; and affection, 47; authors' beliefs concerning, 18; authors' involvement in, 17–18; authors' unique approach to, 9–10; benefits of, 16–17, 43–44; definition of, 22; efficiency of, 47; fears concerning, 29–33; global nature of, 45–48, 172; people's view of, 40–41; popularity of, 47; power of, 15, 39–40; practice for, 17; purpose of, 15, 30; results of, 47; and risk taking, 37–38; as safety net, 37–38; and score keeping, 27–28; self-assessment for, 51–55; time needed for, 32; and two sides of power networking, 41; as way of life, 15–16, 173–174, 184–184; and what networking is not, 22. *See also* Power networking

Networking events: choice of, 122; as opportunity, 125–126; preparation for, 123

Networking mongrels, 21–22, 33, 95

Networking profile, 51–55

Notations on business cards, 96

Notebook, for organizing and retrieving network, 114

Notecards, personalized, 106

Notes: beginnings for, 105; developing habit of regularly sending, 104–105; effect of, 105; nurturing through, 104–105; personalized notecards for, 106
Nurture: with calls, notes, and gifts, 104–105; definition of, 104; of network, 183–184

Obligation, fear of, 30
Open-mindedness, 161, 162
Organization: and retrieval of network, 113–114; of thoughts before phone calls, 120–121. *See also* Self-management
Organizations, professional: committee and board membership in, 147; membership in, 145–146

Participation: action plans and action steps for, 154; case studies of, 151–153; in committee or board responsibilities in professional organization, 147; through membership in professional organization, 145–146; and reevaluating and adding to network, 150; in regularly giving referrals and making requests of network, 148; "three-foot rule" of, 149, 151–152; visibility through, 145–154
Peale, N. V., 118
Personal accomplishments, 61–62
Personal appearance and presentation, 73–74
Personal goals, 65
Personal management. *See* Self-management
Personal power as networker, 64, 167–168
Personal values and principles, 59–60
Personalized notecards, 106
Phone calls. *See* Telephone calls
Pierce, J., 108
Positive feedback. *See* Acknowledgments
Power networking: acknowledgments in, 101–110; action plans and action steps for, 70–72, 90–92, 98–99, 111–112, 127–129, 143–144, 154, 165, 179; and being known as powerful networker, 167–168; benefits of, 169; and business cards, 95–99, 115; case studies of, 67–69, 87–89, 97, 108–110, 124–126, 141–142, 151–153, 162–164, 175–177; and commitment to success of people in network, 156; and committee or board responsibilities in professional organization, 147; and completion of daily action list, 117–119; and conversation generators, 79–80; and decision to attend networking events, 122; definition of, 39–40;

and ease in groups, 79–80; and focus on people as they are introduced, 82–83; at forefront of thinking, 170; global nature of, 45–48, 172; graciousness and courtesy in, 73–92; and high level of service, 157; integrity and professionalism in, 160; and intuition, 155; as lifestyle for success, 183–184; and listening, 158–159; versus Lone Ranger mentality, 23–25, 63–64; and memory recall, 82–83; network diagram of, 66; and nurture, 104–105, 183–184; and open-mindedness, 161, 162; and organization of thoughts before phone calls, 120–121; and personal accomplishments, 61–62; and personal appearance and presentation, 73–74; personal approach to, 155–165; and personal goals, 65, 85, 169; and personal power as networker, 64; and personal values and principles, 59–60; and preparation for networking events, 123; priority of, 170; and rapport, 95–99; and reevaluating and adding to network, 150; and regularly giving referrals and making requests of network, 148; and reintroductions, 81; and requests, 131–144, 148; and return of phone calls within twenty-four hours, 119; role modeling for, 171; and role of host, 84–85; and saying no, 122; self-assessment for, 51–55; and self-introduction, 75–78; and self-knowledge, 59–72; and self-management, 113–130; and system for organizing and retrieving network, 113–114; and thoughtfulness, 101–110; "three-foot rule" of, 149, 151–152; and time management, 116–119; two sides of, 41; and visibility of self and business, 85, 145–154; as way of life, 15–16, 173–174, 183–184. *See also* Networking Power of networking, 15, 39–40
Praise. *See* Acknowledgments
Presentation, personal, 73–74
Principles, personal, 59–60
Procrastination, 118–119
Professional organizations: committee or board responsibilities in, 147; membership in, 145–146
Professionalism: in all interactions and endeavors, 160; and participation in professional organizations, 145–147; in personal appearance and presentation, 73–74
Promotional activities, 85
Pushiness, fear of, 32–33
Putman, A., 22, 157

Rapport, and business cards, 95–99
Raynolds, E., 59, 145
Raynolds III, J. F., III, 59, 145
Reevaluating and adding to network, 150
Referrals, 148
Reintroductions, 81
Rejection, 29–30, 137–138
Repetition, in memory recall, 82
Requests: action plans and action steps for,
    143–144; case study of, 141–142; clarity,
    conciseness, and nondemanding manner of,
    133–134; for contacts, 135–136; and follow-up
    on leads, 137–138; hidden agenda in,
    133–134; regular requests of and referrals to
    network, 148; style of, 133–134; for support of
    others, 131–132; and value of every contact,
    139–140
Retrieval system, for network, 113–114
Risk taking, 37–38
RoAne, S., 79, 93, 94, 95, 106
Robbins, A., 123
Role modeling, for power networking, 171
Rolling Thunder, 160
Rolodex system, for organizing and retrieving
    network, 113
Roman, G., 124

Saying no, 122
Schwartz, D. J., 81
Score keeping, 27–28
Self-assessment, 51–55
Self-introductions: case study of, 87–89; criteria
    for, 75–76; examples of, 76–77; importance of,
    75; practice of, 77–78
Self-knowledge: action plans and action steps for,
    70–72; case studies of, 67–69; and giving up
    Lone Ranger mentality, 63–64; and network
    diagram, 66; of personal accomplishments,
    61–62; of personal expertise, 62; of personal
    goals, 65; of personal power as networker, 64;
    of personal values and principles, 59–60
Self-management: action plans and action steps
    for, 127–129; and business card organization,
    115; case studies of, 124–126; and completion
    of daily action list, 117–119; and decision to
    attend networking events, 122; and organization
    of thoughts before phone calls, 120–121; and

preparation for networking events, 123; and
    procrastination, 118–119; and return of phone
    calls within twenty-four hours, 119; and saying
    no, 122; and system for organizing and
    retrieving network, 113–114; and time
    management, 116–119
Seneca, 84
Service, high level of, 157
"Seven-second syndrome," 76
Sinetar, M., 137, 155
Smith, L., 75
Spiral notebook system, for organizing and
    retrieving network, 114
Stamps, J., 40, 133
Stanford, L., 162
Stevenson, R. L., 182
Support: asking for and using, 9–10, 31, 131–
    132; receiving and accepting, 107; in regular
    requests of and referrals to network, 148

Telecommunications, 46–47
Telephone calls: nurturing through, 104–105;
    organization of thoughts before, 120–121;
    preparation for, 120–121; return of, within
    twenty-four hours, 119
Thoughtfulness, in power networking, 101–110
"Three-foot rule," 149, 151–152
Time management, 116–119, 137
Tognacci, G., 69
Treadmill syndrome, 128–129
Triplett, J. F., 147
Trust, 27–28
Tyger, F., 158

Valdez, D., 125–126
Values: from every contact, 139–140; self-
    knowledge of, 59–60
Visibility: through participation, 145–154; of self
    and business, 85
Vitale, J., 63, 157, 175

Wardrobe, 73–74
Wattles, W. D., 139, 161
Weakness, fear of, 31
Windsor Club, The, 12, 152, 178
Williams, P., 149
Wilson, M., 117

Youngs, B. B., 37, 47, 124, 156, 169

ORDER FORM

Quantity	Publication	Price	Total

***Power Networking: 55 Secrets for
Personal and Professional Success***
by Donna Fisher and Sandy Vilas

	Paperback	$14.95	$ _____
	Hardcover	21.95	$ _____

Audiotapes by Donna Fisher and Sandy Vilas:

	"The Ten Commandments of Networking"	10.95	_____

**QUANTITY
DISCOUNTS
ARE AVAILABLE
ON BULK PURCHASES**

Tax (Texas residents only)   _____

Shipping and handling ($1.50/item)   _____

TOTAL $ _____

Name _____

( )

Company _____ Phone # _____

Address _____ City _____ State _____ Zip _____

MasterCard or VISA # _____ Exp Date _____

Signature _____

To order books or for information about workshops, seminars, presentations, and corporate trainings call the authors at:

Donna Fisher
6524 San Felipe,
    Suite 138
Houston, Texas 77057
1-800-934-9675
Fishernet@aol.com
www.donnafisher.com

Sandy Vilas
P.O. Box 881595
Steamboat Springs, CO
    80488-1595
1-970-870-3302
President@coachu.com
www.coachu.com

The Ten Commandments of Networking

Networking is one of the greatest marketing tools around when it is utilized appropriately, wisely and professionally. The following *Ten Commandments of Networking* have been identified as the building blocks for the powerful utilization of networking as a way of life.

1. Give up the "Lone Ranger" Mentality
2. Honor Your Relationships
3. Acknowledge People
4. Manage Yourself as a Resource
5. Take the Initiative
6. Be Your Own Best PR Person
7. Ask for What You Want
8. Expand Your Horizons
9. Follow the Golden Rule of Networking
10. Network as a Way of Life

To schedule a "Ten Commandments of Networking" presentation for:

❑ A conference
❑ A workshop or seminar presentation
❑ A convention

❑ A sales training
❑ A club or association meeting
❑ A retreat
❑ An awards banquet

Call the authors at:

Sandy Vilas
P.O. Box 881595
Steamboat Springs, CO
80488-1595
1-970-870-3302
President@coachu.com
www.coachu.com

Donna Fisher
6524 San Felipe,
Suite 138
Houston, Texas 77057
1-800-934-9675
Fishernet@aol.com
www.donnafisher.com